Boots
&
Bullets

Rachel N. Cleveland

DEDICATION

In loving memory of my sweet nephew,
Jack Ryan Angel.

86 days on this earth was not enough for us, but we are
comforted knowing you are being held by your amazing
Creator. We will do our best to be brave until we are able
to see you again sweet boy.

We love you forever and miss you always.

October 17, 2018- January 11, 2019

CONTENTS

ACKNOWLEDGMENTS

Billy, you are the greatest example of a victorious Christian soldier I have ever had the privilege of knowing. Thank you for being a constant example of service and truth. I am proud to have worked with you for so long, but now I am ruined forever after having you as the best boss in the world!

And to Damon, this book wouldn't have been possible without you. Not only did you allow me to spend hours peppering you with questions about your military experience, you went on countless adventures with me, and constantly bring joy to my life. Thank you, friend!

1

INTRODUCTION

When I was younger, I wanted to be many things in life. At one time or another, I thought I'd be a teacher, a marine biologist, an opera singer, or even a Disney voice. But at the back of my mind, at the heart of who I was, I always wanted to be in the military. To be a soldier for the country that I love, the place I call home, the land of the free. I wanted to represent this great nation at a crucial time, in a vital role, and do all of it with no one really knowing my name. I wanted my patriotism to surpass singing the national anthem with the conviction of a founding father. I wanted my life to mean something important to this great land, even if it meant laying it down. To this day, I read military novels, love watching war and military movies and shows and get all the feels every time I hear the playing of "God Bless America," all because I love this place and feel very blessed to call it home.

There are very few things in this world I feel this way about. God, my family, a handful of friends I consider family, and this country and the founding principles of honor, prosperity, freedom, and equality that it stands for. Even now, every time I hear of someone who has served, I thank them for their sacrifice and for their dedication to keeping us free. What a love they have shown to millions of people they will never know, see, or hear about. This is why the 4th of July is my favorite holiday. Not only does it have the best food, fun, and fireworks (EEK! I do love me some fireworks!), but it is one of the days we remember the freedoms we hold so dearly and offer thanks to those who have given much, if not all, for those freedoms to be protected.

There have always been things about the military that fascinate me, but one, in particular, stands out: their uncanny ability to do what needs to be done no matter the crisis, situation, region, circumstance, or resources given to them. They just do it. They keep moving forward. They respond to the call and continue until the job is done. Every time. I once heard in a military-themed show, *Shooter,* and later realized they were quoting Tennyson, that the job of the soldier was described as "ours is not to reason why ours is just to do or die." They receive orders, they execute, and then they repeat the process all over again. They don't question, they just do or die trying. Literally. They maintain a wartime mentality at all times. There is no time not to keep this mindset. I wish I were that way. The discipline it requires sounds exhausting! I can't even stick with a TV show for very long before I get bored of the plots or can guess the ending and move on to something else. The longest discipline I have had in my life, other than writing in journals on a regular basis and keeping the job that I love, is wearing a Fitbit every day for the last 2 years. AND THAT STAYS ON ME MOST OF THE TIME, TO BEGIN WITH! (And side note, since the completion of this book I have stopped wearing said

Fitbit because my health goals shifted, and it no longer was helpful in getting me the information I needed to reach those goals. So, there you go. I can't even keep a Fitbit relationship going!)

From the soldiers I know, they have explained how they train day in and day out for the order to come in that calls them to danger. The order that draws them out into the unknown. They give of their lives, their time, and their resources, all for the good of us at home to be safe and happy and healthy. Every time I think of a soldier, I stop and think, "This is what the Lord has called me to be!" At first, I thought the calling was to be an actual soldier, a strong member of any branch of the military. Now, I know He has called me to be a soldier for His army. In 2 Timothy 2:3-4, believers are identified as being in the Army of the Lord, or soldiers for the kingdom.

Being called to be a soldier for Christ looks different every day, just like the life of a soldier is never the same. One minute he is straightening his sheets in the bunk and the next thing he knows he is being called out on a mission with no idea of when he will return to that same bunk. A soldier for Christ is the same. There will be some days where being a soldier means you are following orders and must keep doing what you are doing. I think those are sometimes the boots' days. They can be mundane, repetitive, quiet, but as soldiers, you must still be ready to walk into battle prepared to fight at any moment. So, you continue to keep up with the drills, stay in top shape, and get ready for the next time you are called out to the field. Then there are those days where we are actually at war, and it requires us to pull the trigger, to take great action, and to conquer in the name of Christ. These are the bullets' days. They are not often pretty, but they always have a purpose behind their existence.

But what does all of this even mean? What does it look like to be a soldier for Christ? Why is it so important? And does it actually mean anything to me specifically? Man am I so glad you asked! There is a concept called a wartime mentality. It was first introduced to me through a sermon at the church I attend. My pastor was quoting the great Christian beast, John Piper. In his book, *Don't Waste Your Life*, Piper discusses his memory of wartime life. The way the average person's life changed on a daily basis to accommodate and prepare for the war that was raging nearby or overseas. His words are so earth-shattering to me, I can't NOT let you see them for yourself.

> "I am wired by nature to love the same toys that the world loves. I start to fit in. I start to love what others love. I start to call earth "home." Before you know it, I am calling luxuries "needs" and using my money just the way unbelievers do. I begin to forget the war. I don't think much about people perishing. Missions and unreached people drop out of my mind. I stop dreaming about the triumphs of grace. I sink into a secular mindset that looks first to what man can do, not what God can do. It is a terrible sickness. And I thank God for those who have forced me again and

again toward a wartime mindset." (p. 112)

This quote right here has so changed my thinking I'm not sure my life will ever be the same. We will talk more about that in a later chapter, but between Piper's words here and the ones I quoted in the previous book by Jon Acoff, *Give the Grave Only Bones,* I literally should never have to search for more motivation to get something done, spend the time to love on others, find personal encouragement, and downright stop being lazy. You notice I said, 'should never.' Yeah, about that... I'm still a broken human. I need all the guidance, redirection, wisdom, and clarity I can get. That's just another reason I'm thankful for the love of friends, family, Jesus, and confirmation of His promises through His word. I'm working on it. Slowly.

Before we begin, I must confess I am no expert in military history, strategy, or combat. I don't even look good in a kickboxing class. I am also no expert in God, the Bible, or doing life perfectly for that matter. What I am is a believer in a God that does great and mighty things, with some very underwhelming people. And I think that's what He is doing here when He gave me the desire to write this second book. My first book was about my own life, my own struggles, my own pain and triumph through God's redeeming grace. I like to think this book is more of a journey we can take together, a look at the Word and discussion on what we think it can mean for our lives, and what I think it means for my own life. And above all, I want this book to make you stop and ask yourself, "What does it mean to be living with a wartime mentality for Christ? And am I doing that with every day I'm given?" I hope we can discover this together. Discover what those answers are for you and for me, and how having a wartime mindset for the Kingdom can transform our days, our relationships, and our lives. (And... queue the Star-Spangled Banner. The Boston Pops version is the best in case you wanted to know!)

Part One:

Preparing for Battle

2

WARTIME MENTALITY

In the introduction of this book, I provided a quote from Piper's *Don't Waste Your Life*. I told you the "wartime mentality" concept came from this quote and it 100% did. This whole idea is the foundation of why I felt I needed to write this book. Not just for myself, but for anyone who is seeking to understand more of what it means to be an active participant in the battle that is constantly going on around us. Then once we become active participants what does it mean for us to move forward. How does this information change our lives? Enter, wartime mentality or as Piper calls it "wartime lifestyle".

Before missions take place, training is always needed. We will talk about discipline and the benefits of training in coming chapters, but missions also take reconnaissance, intelligence, maps, and locations in order for soldiers to adequately prepare for whatever they may face. Being mission minded involves using your training and preparation time to the point where everything becomes automatic, habits are built in, and responses are involuntary. Our own spiritual training starts with daily reading of the battle manual God has left for us, the Bible, the sword of the spirit. We will talk more about this specifically in another chapter, but for the purposes of being mission-minded, our Bibles are a central tool to our success. It is the map that allows us to know what direction to go. It is written mission orders for us to follow, for us to obey. The practice of being in the word daily is not always an easy one, but it is essential to the success of our mission. It equips us for the battle ahead.

Another of our tools is each other. We are all brother in arms, encouraging one another. Soldiers know they can depend on their team, their brotherhood, and they are completely secure in their place on that team. These men and women proudly display the flag of the USA on their sleeves. As they prepare to go into battle, these flags serve as a reminder for whom they are fighting for. They wear it boldly on their arms as a mark of their citizenship and their allegiance. The same is true for us as believers. Part of understanding what being mission-minded, or having a wartime mentality, means recognizing where our identity lies and to whom we have placed our allegiance in. And as believers, we are citizens of heaven (Philippians 3:20), coheirs to the Kingdom of God. It means that our hearts are set to the beat of the heavenly drum, and our bodies long to be part of the kingdom for which we were always meant to dwell in. We are siblings in Christ, and our brotherhood is a weapon all its own power.

This community grows out of knowing where we come from and where we are going is a vital part of remaining in the mission mindset, it should also influence everything about how we live. My pastor, Matt Chandler, recently reminded me of this concept.

If our citizenship lies in heaven, this means everything we do is to further the kingdom of God. Our marriages, raising children, our friendships, our jobs. All of it should be focused on and directing us to the kingdom work we have been assigned to do. Being mission minded means we use every area of our life to battle on behalf of our King, always. It means using our finances to further His work, allow our job to be an act of worship, utilizing our conversations and relationships to build up other kingdom warriors.

I don't know about you, but I have to constantly be reminded there is a battle raging on around me. That my job is an area in which I am called to proclaim the name of the Lord. Or that my mission of reaching people does not pause because I have a bad day or too full a schedule. Rather, the battle is constant, and the mission has yet to be accomplished. Therefore, I must get to work. I must love others. I must remember to use every chance I get to encourage other soldiers and help train up new ones. But I'm selfish and forget so many times. God is gracious towards me and continues to give me more opportunities to do better. Thankfully, He doesn't see failure, He sees room for improvement.

Having a wartime mentality should shift the way we live. It should ignite a fire in our souls that nothing and no one can ever extinguish. The sad thing is that it took me a very long time to even figure out I needed to live with a mission mindset and an even longer time to know what that meant let alone live it every day. And I am still working on living that way every day. It requires me to step out of my comfort zone, out of my selfish world and engage in the lives of those around me. It means I have to acknowledge that blood, sweat, and tears are going to be part of my story, and they are there to make me better. A stronger warrior of the faith. A wartime mentality is not just about being on guard, though that is part of it. It is also about knowing what is required of you and accepting the mission laid before you. It means trusting your commanding officer, believing He knows what He is doing. And above all else, it means that you are willing to give your all to complete the mission.

What if you don't have a wartime mentality? What if you don't really see things with urgency or as a mission? How do you change your mind? Wow, you are so smart! What great questions! I am so glad you asked. If you don't have a wartime mentality, I would challenge you to look at a few things, and I'm going to say this as lovingly as possible. First, examine your relationship with the Lord. If you don't have a passion for Him, for His word, for loving His people, I would deeply encourage you to ask for that passion. The Lord is faithful in hearing our prayers and giving us the desires of our heart. And if those don't happen to be on your desires list, there may be other ways of identity and insecurity or selfishness you may need to break down before they can become desires. All of those things I listed are scripture-based callings for all believers. It is not a Christian wish list or good Samaritan checklist. They are characteristics meant to define us as believers so that others may know us by our love (John 13:35). If those desires are missing in life, seek out God's grace in bringing them to your heart. He will do it!

Second, if a wartime mentality is missing from your life, I would ask you to examine your lifestyle and financial situation. Again, both will clearly show what is important to you, how your sense of time is measured, and where your security lies. Here's a small example of what I mean: if I spend 20% of my budget eating out with people, that could give someone the impression I love food, I love my friends, and I invest in spending time with them around good food. None of those things are bad. Seriously, I love me some good Tex-Mex and long conversations with my crew. However, when spending 20% on eating out exceeds the amount of time and money I am investing in the church, in my small group members, in my tithing, and in ministry, I would want someone to ask me about my priorities in life. I would want someone to ask me the hard questions. Like "Is spending money eating out getting you closer to meaningful relationships with friends? With Jesus? Is this time impacting the kingdom?." Hear me when I say, I do NOT get this right all the time. And every second of my day or every penny that I spend is not 100% kingdom based. But I hope I get there one day. I hope I will reach a place in my life where everything I do and every penny, I spend has a purpose that will impact the Kingdom, immediately or eventually.

Maybe that sounds crazy to you. It sounds crazy to me. But what if more people lived this crazy, mission-minded life? What if we all were so Kingdom focused it challenged the way we lived every day? What kind of world would we live in if we all increased our mission-mindedness even 1%? Can you even imagine? Man, revival would breakout. How many more lives would be saved? How many more workers would participate in the harvest? We already know the workers are few (Matthew 9:37). It just gets me so excited to think about a world like that. And I honestly believe we can get there. That I can get there. And it starts with one step towards being mission-minded in our everyday lives.

Lastly, the best way I know how to encourage you to embrace and discover a wartime mentality is for me to give you a stellar example. And the best example of all was Jesus. Jesus lived the ultimate life on a mission. He knew from the very beginning his days were numbered. He knew before he walked his death would come quickly. Can you even imagine living a life that way? Counting down the days instead of counting up. Yet knowing this, he did everything with a purpose. His miracles were intentional. He lived simply so he could invest in others fully. His words were always crafted well in advance. His journey was mapped and laid out before him. He used every day he was given to proclaim his Father to this world, to love others, to disciple his children and to push back the Devil. He knew exactly what was going to be required of him, and he set out to accomplish it. He did not hesitate. He did not back down. Even to death. There on the cross, he proclaimed it all to be done. It was finished. There is literally no better example of a mission-minded person to ever walk this earth. He had approximately 12,045 days to complete his mission, and he didn't waste a single one of them. Jesus set out with the mission in mind and accomplished that mission for our sake, not his. Missions always have a purpose, always have an objective. And we were his.

Our mission, like Christ's, is to use every day as a platform to further the work of the Kingdom. It will require us to "seek justice, love mercy, and walk humbly" (Micah 6:8). It should change the way we live because not only are we children of God, we are citizens of heaven. Our identity is no longer tied to who we are or what we do, but who lives in us. We utilize examples like Jesus to remain aware of the war going on around us, and we keep our focus on the mission. We work hard to keep that warrior mentality, that mission mindset so that we will remain faithful in the fight we are called to. So, mount up warriors. We have our gear to strap on, work to do, and a mission to accomplish.

3
BOOTS

There are many tools and pieces of equipment a soldier uses to accomplish their missions. Some of these articles are for defending themselves against the enemy and others are to protect them as much as possible from threats. Offensive and defensive pieces are taken into battle, and it is the soldier's job to know how and when to use them appropriately. One of the lesser recognized assets soldiers take with them are their boots. While it may sound simple, boots are the foundation of protection for the soldier as they head into battle. Boots protect their feet and give them solid ground on which to stand. They are a vital part of the equipment a soldier is given upon accepting their rank in the military.

In the introduction of this book, I referred to boots as being the days where the Lord has called you to stand firm in the battle. I often think they are the days we are meant to wait on Him, to be still and know that He is God and He is at work (Psalm 46:10). I don't know about you, but these are some of the hardest days for me. I am typically an action-oriented human. I dislike unresolved conflict, I'd rather just have the difficult conversation and get it over with. I am VERY impatient when it comes to some areas of life and waiting on the Lord is 100% one of those areas. Not because I don't trust Him or what He is doing, but because I'm human and we get everything so quickly these days. Thankfully, God is bigger than instant potatoes, computers that fit in our back pockets, and the instant gratification of Google finding all the answers for us. If I have a question I don't know the answer to, I ask Google. And let's be real if Google doesn't know, then is it actually worth knowing??? Just kidding. Google can find everything. And I trust it to give me answers when I need them.

So, if I am so trusting of a computer algorithm, why is it so difficult for me to trust the one who created the minds to put algorithms together in the first place? Ugh.

I want immediate answers, and there are so many times the Lord knows I can't handle immediate answers, or He wants me to learn to trust Him more, or things are still being worked out, and they aren't ready for me yet. Whatever the reason He chooses to have me wait, and it's not just me. Countless people in the Bible spend their lives waiting on the Lord. Abraham waited (albeit not always patiently) for his promised son to come and be the first of a great nation. Job waited for the Lord to restore his life after countless attacks from Satan himself to tear Job down. John the Baptist spent years waiting for Jesus' arrival proclaiming His coming. Lazarus waited dead in a grave for Jesus to come and bring him back to life. Even now, as believers, we eagerly wait for the second coming of Christ when the world will be restored, and there will be no more tears, pain, suffering, or night. Waiting is a beautiful part of how

God has shown His authority, His sovereignty, and His ultimate plan throughout history. So why should I expect Him to do it any differently with me? He is the same, yesterday, today, and forever right? He is constant and always knows what He is doing. Especially in waiting. He is always, always, always in the waiting.

In those boots days, as we are called to wait, we must also know our waiting is not in vain. These days build courage and strength. Every soldier knows the hardest part of being in the battle is waiting for things to unfold, waiting for your ride home, waiting for something to go wrong. But they are never sitting idly as they wait. They are always on guard, always on the lookout for danger, and always ready to take action should it be required of them without notice. Boot days are not lazy days. They are days where we are to be actively engaged in the world around us, with our hearts and minds guarded and our weapons at the ready. Just because we are called to be still at the moment, does not give us the right to be undisciplined, lazy, or unprepared. Rather the opposite, these waiting days should be full of preparation. They are for us to utilize the calm before, and sometimes in, the storm to prepare ourselves for the bullet days that are coming. While waiting is not particularly fun, it is necessary for us to catch our breath and prepare for what lies ahead. We should be thankful for these days, covet them while they are here, instead of wishing them to pass more quickly.

I have been guilty of wishing away these waiting days recently. I was in a season of waiting. I had just passed through a season of battle, and with the Lord's gracious faithfulness I have weathered the storm. And now that there was less action going on around me, fewer bullets flying, I found myself wishing to be out of the quieter season I found myself in and moving on to the next step He has for me, the next chapter. I caught myself praying for the waiting to be over and the new to come. I thought I was ready to face whatever is next. Obviously, I wasn't. I was worn out from the fight I had just endured, and I needed this waiting season to allow my heart to heal, to restore my trust in the Lord as He provided for me, and to build up my reserves again. How can I go to battle if I was replete of all my resources? These boots days were vital to my human heart to heal, and my spiritual body to build up strength for the next mission. This idea of waiting but still building for the future is something my church calls an "already but not yet" mentality. It is where you anticipate the vision of the future, what the Lord is working towards, but are still very much doing your best to live in the present. You must stand still and wait for the Lord to display His majesty before your eyes (1 Samuel 12:16).

You see when we are mission-minded, sometimes this stops us from living, if not thriving, in the present situation we are in. This is what makes my wishing away the waiting process so destructive. Not wanting to be in the waiting season, hoping for the boot days to pass quickly, often makes me miss out on the people, learning, and beauty around me in the present. And I never want to be someone who isn't present in their own life. I don't want to miss the amazing blessings the Lord has given to me, the mercies made new each morning, the beautiful creation around me. I don't want to miss time with family or friends, because I'm so anxious to move on to the next phase of life. I want to thrive in the now as I prepare for what is to come. Boot days are critical for preparation, but they should also be valued as a beautiful reminder to be thankful for where you are. In your own waiting, stand firm, take courage and hold on. He is giving you time to heal and is preparing you for the next mission, one where boots, a crucial part of your equipment and armor (Ephesians 6:11) will be required for a successful outcome. And as you wait, know that He is fighting for you. You need only to be still (Exodus 14:14).

Take courage my heart, Stay steadfast my soul
He's in the waiting, He's in the waiting

Hold onto your hope, as your triumph unfolds
He's never failing, He's never failing

-Bethel Music, *Take Courage*

4
BULLETS

Ok, confession time. I have been afraid to write this chapter since the idea of this book began in the smallest corners of my mind. When I set out to write a book about living a warrior life, I felt like a fraud. I still do, honestly. I often don't think of myself as brave or strong, and I think those are prime characteristics of what it takes to be a warrior. I've been afraid to write this bullets chapter because it is about taking action. I thought once I had a big event in my life or a big change, it would require me to make a difficult decision, then I would be better equipped to write this chapter. I have been waiting for that moment pretty consistently for the last six months or so. Wondering when and how the Lord was going to ask me to take action. Then today happened.

Today I am nearing the end of spring break at our university. It has been a busy week at the office, though no students have been on campus. We have been planning for the future, purchasing large items for the end of year events, and working to get new team members up to speed on the program. It has been wonderfully busy, joyfully exhausting, and amazingly energetic. Thankfully I was able to take a day or two off this week in an effort to recharge before the end of the semester begins, and the hectic chaos enters into my life over the next eight weeks. I was working from home today and had just completed my email replies and some additional work items for the day. With everything put away, I went to read through a study my small group is doing on Hebrews by N.T. Wright. We are going through the entire book together this semester and are on the 6th chapter of Hebrews for tonight's study. I read through the chapter in the Bible and then the commentary and questions provided by Wright. He asked some thought-provoking questions which encouraged me to see this chapter of scripture in a different way.

Finally, I arrived at the last paragraph of the chapter, and I stopped. At the end of the chapter, Wright offers some extra notes on Hebrews 6:9-12. His comments centered around the concept of grace. Since the Reformation, he mentions, Christians have rightly been taught that nothing we do can earn God's love. Which is 100% true. Nothing we ever do will get us to heaven, prove we are worthy to be there, or impact our status once we get there. Nothing but a relationship with Jesus. But then Wright goes on to point out while this is true, the New Testament speaks many times to the things we do as Christians and how what we do actually do matter. It matters a lot. Here's what he says,

> "Yes, there are undoubtedly times
> when, like the children of Israel beside
> the Red Sea, we need the message that
> says, 'The Lord will fight for you; all

you need to do is to be still' (Exodus 14:14). But those are the exceptional moments, the particular situations, often in times of emergency, when there is nothing we can or should do, and we must trust that God will do it all. But the normal Christian life is one of energy, enthusiasm, faithful effort, and patient hard work."

Those exceptional moments are the boots days. The ones we talked about in the previous chapter. The others, the ones Wright refers to as the normal Christian life, are the bullet days. Did you catch that? Our normal Christian life is meant to be one of action, of hard work. Being one of action doesn't just mean on the big decision days like I thought would be required of me to write this chapter. No, bullet days are the normal days of putting in hard work for the Kingdom. It comes from God working through us with the power of the Holy Spirit (Philippians 2:12-13). It made me stop to think that my normal days are bullet days in the eyes of the

Lord. I don't think they are bullet days. I think they
are normal, mundane, and honestly sometimes
boring. I can be a completely BORING person. I
know you are so shocked by that, but I'm cool with it.
I enjoy being alone and with people. I enjoy having
no plans and catching up with my shows on Hulu, by
myself. I also enjoy being around great people,
especially if I get to wear comfy sweatpants at the
same time!

Bullet days, Wright is suggesting are the
ordinary days when we make "faithful effort and
patient hard work" to further the name of Christ.
They are the days we are fighting the good fight and
taking action that has eternal benefits, one baby step
forward at a time. These days may not have a great
deal of progress, but the fact is forward is still
progress. I don't know about you, but that completely
changes the way I look at my "normal" day. I thought
the normal days were the boots days. Me just trucking
along until a crisis or life situation hits me and then I
had to take action, I had to pull the trigger so to
speak. But instead, now I actually think bullet days are

when we dig in and do the dirty parts of life well with a kingdom perspective. When we have meaningful conversations with the student we are mentoring, when we get the opportunity to serve others with a grateful heart, when we offer others grace instead of hostility or judgment, when we use our resources and energy to help push back injustice, when we dispense our energy to love our children, spouses, families, and friends well. These are bullet moments, friends. They may be disguised as ordinary life situations or calls, but these are the bullets we must fire into the world to push back the darkness. These are the moments that require us to truly invest, not just listen and move on. They are the times we have to be vulnerable, give of ourselves, and be willing to forego our own selfish desires in order to be fully present at the moment we are in. These are the dirty and difficult moments that make up our ordinary lives.

Digging into these kinds of moments is hard, but we are given a choice. We can flee from it or fight for it. The classic situation of fight or flight. Within the last six months, I have started taking kickboxing classes, which I LOVE! But from this experience, I am faced every day with the decision to fight or flight, usually before I ever even get to the door. First, I have to decide if I'm going to go to class at all. Do I go in and fight for my inner and outer strength? Or do I run as far from the studio as possible? Which also usually means run to get tacos! Thankfully most of the time, my fighting side of the brain wins, and I go to class. Once I'm inside, I am surrounded by fighters. It is such an amazing feeling walking in that place and being greeted by people of all shapes and sizes fighting hard for a lifestyle they want. It is so encouraging to see people choose to fight, for themselves, for others, whatever their reason for being there is, it is inspiring. Then all of us who have decided to fight that day, actually get to the hard part of fighting. We condition, we throw punches, we kick bags, and we do partner drills. That's right, after making the hard decision to just show up, I have to then actually put in the sweat to do the training. This whole fighting thing is HARD! But digging in, fighting instead of escaping, doing the hard work is worth it. It's the only way anyone ever sees results in anything.

I wish I could tell you I choose to fight every time life gives me a choice, but I don't. The Lord graciously gave me the personality that rarely backs down, often doesn't mind doing the hard work, but I am not perfect nor am I Wonder Woman. There are plenty of times I choose flight instead of fight. There are times I just don't want to fight for what I think, believe, or want. I get tired. I get tired of fighting and walking away seems easier. Sometimes walking away is the better answer, but not if it means you are walking away from your life. What I mean is, Paul continually talks to Christians in the New Testament about working hard, about plowing, harvesting blessing after the hard work of planting has been done. We can't expect a good harvest in life if we continually choose to not participate in the work required of us. Yet, we are selfish people and have to fight against our flighty tendencies all the time. Myself included.

We have to challenge ourselves to fight the lazy Christian life, even just the regular lazy life. We have to fight for good relationships with our families, for healthy friendships, for a meaningful relationship with God. We have to take action against the darkness that is continuing to creep into our homes, our churches, and our lives. We cannot just sit ideally by and let our laziness determine our outcome. Because that outcome keeps us from experiencing abundant living, deep connection to our Creator, and joyful Kingdom work. No, this life requires us to see our days as more action-oriented than we may think, more bullet days in our calendars rather than boot days. Both are part of our journey, but those bullet days should be our norm. And guess what, when you are living with a wartime mentality your normal becomes those bullet days. Ask any soldier who was deployed to a war zone, and they will tell you their "normal" daily soundtrack was full of bullets flying and bombs booming. What was abnormal was quiet and usually quiet meant something bad was going to happen. Like that eerie quiet before the storm hit. So maybe it is time for us to take these days of hard work and think of them as days of action. Maybe it is time we start looking at the mundane as rages of war against the enemy. Maybe, just maybe, it is time for us to dig in and make bullet days out of our new normal. Because then we may be able to see what all the Lord will be able to do with soldiers who are taking their assignment seriously. Who's with me? Oorah.

5
WINNERS AND LOSERS

In every game or every battle, there is a winner and a loser. Usually, when you start out, neither side knows which will win, but both are wanting the victory. In games, winners are easily distinguished. They earn the most points, have the best time, or go the longest distances. In war, however, victory has different definitions. While a treaty or agreement may be met in the end, the death toll for each side, the debt incurred, or the resources now made scarce impact both sides. Victory doesn't always seem like a winning word when it comes with such loss associated with it.

In our battle, we are given the benefit of knowing the outcome already. We are guaranteed victory! Scriptures tell us Jesus gets the final say in how this earth ends. And this earth, as we know it, does end. Revelations make that very clear. With us knowing the end result, why do we have to battle at all? To reveal the glory of God to others (John 11), that they may come to know Him as their own Savior and be part of the final victory. Since the end is already known, maybe we should better understand the fight we are in. I think understanding those that play major roles in battle are important to know.

Jesus has the most impactful role in the battle we find ourselves in. He's the Hero of the story. The final victor left standing in the arena. He faces every type of enemy, temptation, and trial there is and comes out spotless, the perfect Savior. Throughout the bible we see him described as advocate, author and perfecter of our faith, bread of life, bridegroom, deliverer, good shepherd, Great High Priest, faithful and true, light of the world, the one who sets us free, redeemer, our hope and peace, resurrection and the life, wonderful counselor, prince of peace. And that is just a few of the many, many names and descriptors of Jesus. He is fully God and fully man. He is a son, brother, teacher, and friend. Knowing who Jesus is, our commanding officer, can help us in the midst of battle. Because we know him, we can trust him. We can trust when He gives us orders, direction, advice. We know His plans will ultimately lead to victory and to our good and His glory. The more you know about your commanding officer, they more willing you are to obey their objectives, trust their perspective, and give your life to their cause. I only pray you have the right commanding officer leading you into battle. I pray it is Jesus because He is the only winning side and the only loving side in this war.

Now that we know the winner, maybe we should take a minute to look at the enemy. Soldiers never go into a mission without an objective. They also never go into a situation without being able to identify who the friendlies and enemies are. If you haven't guessed our enemy yet, I'll help you out. Our enemy and the loser of this entire thing is Satan. You would think with already knowing the outcome he would just give up, but apparently, he is arrogant enough to think his efforts aren't completely in vain. There are many names in scripture that describe this fallen angel. Here are a few: the devil, Lucifer, ruler of the demons, god of this world, prince of the power of the air, roaring lion, serpent, dragon, adversary, the tempter, or the wicked one. He is the epitome of darkness and despair. He is manipulative, vindictive, and sly. He is the sleaziest kind of being, waiting to swindle anyone the moment they show any hint of vulnerability. He is a liar and a cheat and will stop at nothing to add troops to his cause. He even tried to tempt Jesus! I mean how arrogant can you be?

It is wildly important for us to know who we are fighting against. Knowing what the enemy is capable of will help us know how best to combat his efforts. But I want to say this as lovingly as possible, our enemy is the Devil, not our fellow man. People, no matter their religious or political beliefs, no matter how difficult to handle, or wounded and brokenhearted, or even sometimes not very nice are

not our enemy. Our war is not with them. They are
our brothers and sisters. We are meant to contend
with them in order to display Christ more clearly to
them. I think sometimes we forget this. I think we
forget that "our struggle [battle] is not against flesh
and blood, but against the rulers, against the
authorities, against the powers of this dark world and
against the spiritual forces of evil in the heavenly
realms" (Ephesians 6:12). This doesn't mean we have
to get along with every person we ever encounter.
This DOES mean we are to show others respect and
grace because they are made in the likeness of God,
they are also His creation, and as such we must treat
them accordingly.

I think sometimes we get caught up in taking
sides instead of standing with the side of humanity.
Someone always wants to be right, which
systematically makes the other person wrong. Yes,
there are definitely specific things that are called out
to be right and wrong in scriptures. But even Jesus
put aside all the rights and wrongs listed to sum them
up with two commands: love God and love others. In

Matthew 22: 37- 40, Jesus proclaims the greatest commandments are to love God with all our hearts, soul and minds, and to love our neighbors as ourselves. He didn't say to love only those who agree with you or love only people you are related to. He said to simple love others. ALL peoples. These beautiful (and maybe sometimes frustrating) creations of God are not our enemy. We must keep that in mind, as we want to stay on alert for when the real enemy comes lurking.

I did not go into as much depth as I would like on the names of Jesus and even the capabilities of the Devil. That could be so many books in and of themselves. I'm using this chapter more as a means to point out the necessity for us to know who and what we are dealing with. For us to go into battle confidently, we must know intimately who we are taking directions from and fighting alongside. We must know Christ, continuing to know Him better every day. We must also know who the true enemy is. We have to be acutely aware of the tactics the Devil uses to try and delay the ultimate victory that is

Christ's. No matter what Satan does he cannot win, but he will try everything in his book to make you think he can. Understanding what he is capable of is critical for us to know then how to combat him. I strongly encourage you to seek out additional resources on these topics. Stick with textbooks or concordance type of references that are scripturally based. I'm not suggesting we all go out and study demons or evil powers. I am saying we need to use the Bible as our foundation to understand the enemy.

6
OUR MISSION

From those who I know in the military, they
have told me every soldier has a mission. They train
for months, if not years, by doing their best to pass
evaluations that make sure they are prepared for their
assignments. As soldiers in the Lord's army, we have
a very clear mission. If you have any background in
the church, you will recognize the passage of scripture
known as the Great Commission, Matthew 28:16- 20.
These verses lay out Christ's final words to His
disciples and charge them with the mission to reach
the nations for His namesake. Just as this mission was
given to the disciples, so it has been given to us. Our
sole purpose on this earth is to share the good news

with everyone, reaching the very far corners of the world, and make His name famous. Just one mission to accomplish. Sounds easy, right? Wrong. If it were easy, it would be done already, with all persons knowing and believing in the free gift of salvation found in Christ, the Savior of the world. But if you look at the end of these verses, you also see that He promises to be with us, even to the end of the age.

When I read this passage, I get excited and nervous. I mean "making disciples of all nations" is a big job. It sounds so daunting. How in the world will I be able to do that? All the nations? Like ALL of them? Yes, of course, the Savior of the world actually wants to save ALL the world. Crazy to think, I know. (Please tell me you hear my humor in this statement? No? Just me?) This section of the gospel is so exciting because this means the Lord has great plans for this world, and He wants us to be a part of it! This also makes me nervous because it feels like a very big task some days. Thankfully we are not alone in this mission, we have each other, and the Lord left us the Holy Spirit to convict and draw hearts to Himself.

Our job is to plant the seed, tend the field, and be workers of the harvest (Luke 10:2).

I don't know how it has been for you, but winning souls for the Kingdom isn't the easiest thing for me. I have never been the best person to walk up to someone and ask them if they know Jesus as their personal Savior. I am, however, someone if asked why I believe in Jesus, I have an answer and am happy to answer questions to the best of my ability. What I have found to draw people to the love of Christ is to be Jesus to them in my everyday life. To love people as best as I can, to show kindness and support of others, to celebrate life and hardships alongside others, and to stay true to my beliefs in the midst of a wildly turbulent environment. I try to be the light in a very dark and twisted world, for the Light is in me, and I can't not show it to those around me. He is a part of my very existence. And it is always my prayer that when they see me, they are really seeing a reflection of Him.

Hear me when I say, I don't just leave my actions alone to speak the gospel to those around me.

No, there are many times words are actually needed. And in those moments, I pray for wisdom and for the Holy Spirit to take over and for the goodness of the good news to be the message that is spoken. Even though I know I am to proclaim Jesus to all, it isn't always easy for me. But I try. I keep trying because I have faith enough to believe the God that created all things can use this lowly created being in ways I cannot understand. He can most certainly use the timid words and awkward moments to make His name known, opening the hearts of many. For those of you who see this mission as something much easier than I described I want you to know, I am so thankful for people like you. While we are all called to spread the news, there are some with a gift of teaching that are able to more eloquently speak truth to the world than I am. You inspire me, and I know that God is using you in extraordinary ways, just as He is using me and my gifts in other ways.

The great thing about this mission is that we aren't in it alone. Just like a team of soldiers, they all have their assignments. Each is an expert in their own skill set, and still, they are cross-trained and capable of covering for one another. In the same way, we get a whole crew of people to help us. A team of believers each with different gifts and abilities to love others through. We don't have to depend on our own strength. We get to depend on the body of believers along with Christ himself. This mission is not laid upon my shoulders only. Instead, it is the eternal mission of the church until Christ returns. I don't know about you, but having a team makes me feel so much more encouraged. Not only does Jesus remind us He is with us to the end of the age, but He has also given us each other to battle together and accomplish the mission. There will be days the mission seems to be going well, and other days when it seems as if you haven't gained an inch of footing. In those days, take the hand of the soldier next to you, breath deep, and remember you are not alone. You have each other, the Holy Spirit, and God himself are all present cheering you on as you fight to complete the mission of bringing others to Jesus for themselves.

Every time I think of someone successfully

completing a mission, I have the image of Olympians coming in first place. They have their hands in the air, huge smiles on their face, and this exuberant presence. They have worked their whole lives for that one moment. They did it! They won. All their hard work has paid off, their medal is waiting, and the world will know their name. Guess what friends, we have a moment just like this waiting for us. But bigger. That's right. When our mission is done, when we cross the finish line, we will have won. We will have our arms raised in worship, smiles on our faces and an air of exuberance around us because we will be in the presence of the Great Victor. He will look at us and present us with our medals, our crowns, and He will know our names. Good and faithful servant (Matthew 25:23) He will call us as He welcomes us into the greatest party this world has never seen. As you fight this battle, remember your mission. It isn't all about working on being a better Christian, rather our main mission is about being better at sharing Christ's love with all the nations until we cross that finish line into victory.

7

LEADERSHIP

I teach college students and corporate mentors about leadership every day. I have studied a variety of leadership theories, designed curriculum around the concept of leadership, and given countless presentations on the topic around the world. It is literally in my job description. But when I sit down to write about leadership itself, it is never theories I think of or talks, it's people. When I think of leadership, be it good leadership or bad, someone pops into my head. Because at the heart of leadership one must know it is not always about the actions, the speeches, or the theories, but the person themselves. It is what is inside of the person and how they use that to influence others, support teams around them, and lead well.

One picture of good leadership is my current boss, Billy Johnson. He is the epitome of the BEST boss in the world. We work extremely well together, have been through some very great days and very low days. And through everything, he has reached a place in my life where I lovingly call him my work dad. He is a great person, and that has helped him to be a great leader. He wouldn't tell you he's a great person, but humility is one of his many virtuous qualities. He would tell you though, it took him a long time to learn how to do life well, living as the man God wanted him to be. He constantly reminds me of how fortunate I am to have learned so much at a young age. And in turn, remind him I don't feel like I know anything. We have decent banter about it and then continue on with our work for the day. I say all of this to say, I have learned from Billy what it looks like to be a good leader, not just what it means. What being a good leader looks like is sitting down with your team members and hearing their heart on their lives, their work, the good and the bad. Being a good leader looks like reminding your team to take days off when they have overworked that week, making sure they enjoy and take their vacation time; it looks like standing up for your people, investing in their lives, and giving them the space to be creative in their roles. These are just a few of the many lessons on leadership I have learned from 5 and a half years of working alongside my work dad.

But what makes leadership so important in helping us as we prepare for the battle? As you are gearing up for a mission, don't you want to know who is leading you into the field? Wouldn't it be something of interest to you to know what kind of character they have, or their method of operation, ethical code, or perhaps their success rate? Who you are following in life, in marriage, in your career, or in battle is important. It could very well be the difference between life and death. Thankfully for us as believers, we have an extraordinary leader to be following, a prime example. He is King Jesus. He reigns over our lives through the cross He died on. He serves us daily through His character, His love, and His power. He provides for us, listens to us, guides us and gives us wisdom. He has graciously allowed us along for the ride of life. He leads into battle with victory already in hand, giving us full confidence in where we are going.

He is the opposite of what the world expected a king to be, from the wrong family, and the wrong race. And yet, He captivated our hearts through His love and kindness, His servant's heart. This is what a real leader is, a servant. Mark 10:42- 45 explains this better than I ever could, "And Jesus called them to him and said to them, "You know that those who are considered rulers of the Gentiles lord it over them, and their great ones exercise authority over them. But it shall not be so among you. But whoever would be great among you must be your servant, and whoever would be first among you must be a slave of all. For even the Son of Man came not to be served but to serve, and to give his life as a ransom for many." Even our King of Kings came to serve, to lead, to give his life for others. That is true service, true leadership, true love. Jesus willingly took His call to duty, which lead him to a bloody cross, and then to a victorious resurrection.

Before you head into any war, personally, professionally, or spiritually, you better know who you are following, who is in command. I pray you know our Leader, that you know Him personally, that you have experienced His unbelievable love for you and enjoyed the deep freedom that comes from realizing His sacrifice for you on the cross. It is only through this personal relationship with our Leader that our selfishness lessens and we are ever capable of getting to a place where we can take instruction and guidance from Him, what some would call our marching orders. Every soldier is given tasks to complete from their commander. If Jesus is our commander, our Team Captain, our Leader, then we will have orders to complete. We will have things that need doing to help our efforts in the mission ahead. Not that tasks are required of us to be part of the victory, rather we accomplish tasks (or produce fruit if you want the scriptural word for it) as a byproduct of our service, a response to our obedience and commitment to our Leader. He already has the victory, but that does not mean the battle is over. It means the battle must still be endured, and we all have a part to play, a mission to accomplish. So, I strongly encourage you to get to know your Commander in Chief. I pray you will know Him, and His servant's heart better than you know the plot line of your favorite TV show. Get to know the One who is forever by your side, fighting on your behalf, and leading you into victory over your past, your present, and your future battles.

8
DISCIPLINE

Before all else, discipline seems to be the most important aspect of being a soldier. It is why they spend so much time drilling basics into their heads at boot camp and ultimately what ends up saving many of their lives in the long run. Discipline is the repeated practice of habits, methods, or skills. So that when the time comes, the discipline which is so ingrained in your mind becomes your autopilot taking over your senses in your moment of need.

Discipline is something I am great at in some areas of life, but not as awesome in others. It's almost as if my mind has a limit to how many disciplined areas I can handle. I realize this isn't true, more my own mind being ridiculous. But don't you ever NOT want to be disciplined in everything? Don't you ever just want to have one area of life that you aren't intentional in? No? Just me? Ok cool. Thanks, guys. But in all seriousness, I think I'm a decent, disciplined person. I juggle multiple schedules, friends, family, activities, and without discipline in how effectively I use my time, I would not be able to juggle all of these things. What areas are you good with discipline? Are you one of those people who can go to the gym no matter how you feel because you know you need to keep it up? (I hate you if you are. Just kidding. You are loved... I guess. Ha.) Can you stay with a reading plan for a whole year? Can you stick with a diet even when you don't see results quickly? Or worse, when those delicious cupcakes are sitting in front of you begging you to dig into them? If that sentence alone made you stumble, my bad. Forgive me and let me just say, HANG IN THERE- YOU CAN DO IT!

Discipline is closely related to routine or having a system in place. The difference comes in the purpose behind the act. Discipline comes with drive, intentionality, doing something on repeat for the sake of improvement. Routine, however, is doing something over and over again because it is comfortable for you, it typically lacks concentration or motivation for you to complete the act. It is subtle, but the difference is there. Knowing what this looks like in your own life is vital to you becoming the soldier for Christ you are meant to be. It is not just about being comfortable. It is about working towards something with purpose, motivation, and never quitting.

When I think about the different things we could be disciplined in for the purpose of being a soldier of the Lord, the list could be endless. However, if you think about it in terms of what an actual soldier does, the list gets very simple all of a sudden. Here is what being a soldier is: never quitting, being someone of moral character, being strong and courageous, always having your partner's back. Also, it is keeping your word, never letting go, being someone who will lead the way, training hard, being prepared for any terrain or circumstance, willing at all times to lay down your life for the good of others, and understanding your actions may redeem someone else's life.

Now when I read these as a normal person, a civilian if you will, it is intimidating and somewhat exhausting. But when I put on my God-colored glasses, I see 1 Corinthians 13: 4-8a at its finest (Love is patient, love is kind. It does not envy, it does not boast, it is not proud. It does not dishonor others, it is not self-seeking, it is not easily angered, it keeps no record of wrongs. Love does not delight in evil but rejoices in the truth. It always protects, always trusts, always hopes, always perseveres. Love never fails. - NIV). I see the enactment of Philippians 4:13 (I can do all things through Christ who gives me strength. – NIV). And the living out of John 15:13 (There is no greater love than to lay down one's life for one's friends. –NLT). When I put being a soldier in the context of scriptures, I see this is exactly aligned with how God has created us to live in community with one another, and to bring about the work of his kingdom. We are to be soldiers of love, strength, and sacrifice to a lost and broken world. Discipline is one avenue that helps us get there. And for those of you, like me, still feel it is impossible here is my encouragement to you: it is possible to be a disciplined person, because you are created in the image of the Most High God. You were designed with discipline in mind. He made you able to achieve great things through intentionality and grace. And He will equip you to see it through. Believe this truth and keep putting one foot in front of the other. Keep reading the Bible one chapter at a time. Keep going to the gym. Keep pushing your comfortable limits for the furthering of the gospel of Christ.

9
MONEY AND STUFF

Are you someone who keeps everything?
Someone who continues to purchase new clothes or
shoes and never really gets rid of anything? Someone
who is overly sentimental about random items that
add no value to your current stage of life? Me too! Or
well, I used to be. And then something started to
change. I started to see all these things as just stuff
that I didn't really need, didn't really have space for
nor the desire to look at over and over again. The
Lord was leading me toward a lifestyle of balance and
having so much stuff was weighing me down.

Every once in a while, the Lord nudges me to

reevaluate the things I have in my life. Over the last few weeks, His nudges have returned. When these occur, I am led to my closet and encouraged to stare down all the things that pack it. Clothes, shoes, suitcases, bags, books. Whatever is within those walls (or drawers sometimes), He asks me to reexamine them and ask myself if it is really necessary. This most recent nudge had me going through every closet, drawer, and shelve I have in my apartment. To purge my life of things that were just sitting there collecting dust. Knowing He asks this of me every so often, I have adopted a rule: if I haven't looked at, thought about it, or worn it in the last year (because you have to account for the seasons) then it is time to pass it on to someone else or donate it. I have given clothes and accessories to friends, family, anyone who is interested in taking clothes off my hands.

This purging concept has started to invade the way I look at my finances as well. Am I spending my resources on things that matter? Am I being a good steward of all the Lord has entrusted to me? And that question is really the crux of the matter. That is why the Lord continues to bother me over all the things I have in my life, material and monetary. Because I believe He is continuing to work out in me this beautiful life He has prepared for me. And maybe I just need less baggage so that I can more freely go where He wants me to go, whenever it is that He calls me to do so. That right there is freeing to me.

When a soldier readies themselves for deployment, they know all they will have is a locker or a footlocker to store their gear, clothes, toiletries, and any personal belongings. Everything they need and hold dear fits in a locker. Talk about cutting down on the stuff! But they know it is for their benefit if they go with only the essentials. Having extra things will literally weigh them down because sometimes they have to carry everything with them and other times, they have to move it around to make room for something else. Therefore, the less they have, the less mess they have to manage. I don't know about you, but half of me finds the idea of fitting my life into a cage intimidating and the other half of me thinks it would be so freeing!

I'm not saying you need to go and get rid of everything you own, but if the Lord is calling you to do so then you most definitely should! What I'm saying is, if we are really to live in a wartime mentality shouldn't that affect how we manage our finances? Our resources? If we are actually living with the mindset of the Lord's kingdom is coming, wouldn't we be more prone to give to others? To reduce what we have for the sake of the significance it can make to the cross? How much would we take to put in our locker? Every time I think of this concept, I think of the parable Jesus tells of the man wanting to follow him. He tells the man to leave all he owns and possesses and come follow Christ now. The man was saddened because he had a large amount of wealth and possessions. The things he had back at home were literally keeping him from following the Savior of the Universe (Matthew 19: 16-30). I pray this is never the story about me or my life.

This periodic purging helps remind me of how richly blessed I am, how much the Lord has given me, and just how much I don't need in life.

Don't get me wrong. I am still sentimental, and I keep a few tokens of memories. But I don't keep everything. I love traveling. I've learned when I am there the best token for me to remember the trip are the photos, a piece of artwork, and some kind of jewelry. Things I use, can look at, and can make me smile throughout the day just by looking at it. If you visited my apartment, you would see a huge gallery of artwork on the living room wall. There are photos and paintings from all over the world, none overly expensive, but beautiful and memorable to me. Annie Downs in her book *Looking for Lovely* calls them tokens of remembrance. These are important pieces of our history.

How much is too much? How much is enough? Everyone's answers to those questions are going to be different. Me? I would be happy living in a tiny home of 250 square feet and have the ability to travel wherever and whenever I want. But maybe that's not you. And that's ok. However, I do challenge you to look at your life. Do you have too much stuff weighing you down, physically and emotionally? Is there ever going to be enough "stuff" in your life that will make you happy, successful, or peaceful? I hope you know, the answer to that last question is no. There will never be enough, outside of Jesus, that makes you happy. He is it. Nothing else will fill your life with purpose. Everything else comes with obligations and weight. Not freedom. But loving Jesus and having Him reign in your life does come with freedom.

So, what does this mean? Should you sell everything you own? Maybe. Maybe purging is something you should consider. I'm not saying you need to live in a tiny house as I may get to one day. I am saying, if you have so much that keeps you weighed down, will you be able to go and seek when the Lord tells you to go and seek? Will you rid your life of anything that keeps you from following the Lord with freedom? This could be physical, material things, people, debt, or anything that binds you to this world rather than to the one Christ has called you to be a part of. And that should be a big deal to any believer. A big enough deal to affect the way you see your resources, your finances, and the blessings the Lord bestows upon you in this life. What then my friends, is in your locker? And is it drawing you closer to God or further away?

Part 2:

Weapons of a Warrior

10
SELF-DEFENSE

Now that we have an idea of what different ways to see the war raging around us, I think it is important to understand some of the pieces of equipment that help us fight the battle. All of the tools Paul encourages us to use are for us to defend ourselves with against the enemy. They are defensive and offensive instruments. Utilizing these resources is essential for us as soldiers to continue in the fight, and ultimately to accomplish our mission. We must equip ourselves as best as possible and know that Jesus is always with us. It is kind of weird to say self-defense in this context because it really isn't self. It really isn't just up to me to defeat the enemy. Thank goodness! Maybe we should think of it more as God's defense. He is the one who will ultimately bring about the victory, He is just lovingly letting us be part of it. How cool is that? We get to be part of the victory. In sharing in His victory though, we know that also means we share in His hurts, His compassion for others, His mission to bring all to know Him.

In this day, you learn self-defense as a way to take care of yourself should something happen. You hope you will never have to use it, but you learn it just in case. This same idea is not true of the battle we fight. Our battle is guaranteed. It was started long before we stepped into uniform and will continue long after we have joined God in heaven. So, these defenses are not just in case we need them. They are because we WILL need them. When you read Ephesians 6:10-18, you will see Paul says to put on the full armor of God so that we can take our stand against the devil and that when the day of evil comes, we will be ready. He doesn't say if we find ourselves needing to take a stand against the devil. There is not an if, it is a when. WHEN we take our stand against the devil. It is part of our calling.

There are going to be trials, torture some days. Not because our Father doesn't love us, but because He is making himself known. He is crafting us the only way we will listen, the hard way. We don't learn with quick fixes. Sadly, we require a long process. Just look at your kids (if you have kids) when you are trying to teach them a lesson. Do you know any parent that only tells their kid something one time and they are corrected forever? No. Parents have to repeat themselves again and again. Over long months and maybe even some years, it may finally start to click with your kids. As adults, we like to think we have outgrown that process, but we haven't. We know vegetables are good for us, we know working out is a benefit for us, we know riding around without a helmet isn't safe, we know speeding is not only illegal but irresponsible. And we (I!) do it anyway. It doesn't matter how many speeding tickets we have received or how many times we have fallen and been hurt. We do the wrong thing all the time. So, the Lord gives us lessons. He lovingly lets us be disciplined, be stretched in faith, and be molded into the likeness of His Son. Trials are more often than not required for us to learn. I keep praying this won't always be the case with me. That one day I may actually be mature and get something without 20 million lessons.

Therefore, for all the trials and battles ahead, learn your self-defense well. Understand why buckling the belt of truth around yourself is so important. Examine why you need a breastplate of righteous, or why knowing the gospel offers you an opportunity for a peaceful foundation. Learn what it means to pick up a shield of faith and to have a helmet of salvation placed over our minds. And of course, our sharpest weapon of all, it is essential to know how to wield our swords, the Word of God itself. Before a soldier heads into battle, they assess their gear. They make sure everything is in place, fits properly, and most of all they inspect their weapons. They don't want to be on the battlefield trying to clean their guns. Or have ill-fitting armor meant to protect them. We must do the same as warriors of Heaven. 2 Corinthians 10: 4 reminds us where these tools come from, and the power they have, "for the weapons of our warfare are not of the flesh but have divine power to destroy strongholds." We must know our weapons well, keep them sharp, and understand when to use what piece of armor.

There are some great studies and commentaries out there on the armor of God. I've consulted many of them when researching for this book. Dig into them. It is your job to know what you are working with, so you know which tool to use at the appropriate time. This requires time and dedication. You may not be someone who has the ability to give 3 hours a day to study scriptures. Don't worry. I don't either. But we have to start somewhere. Start with 10 minutes or read 5 pages in a scripture-based study. Give yourself grace but keep moving forward. Keep building your arsenal. These tools are not temporary, they are eternal. They will only be more glorified in heaven.

Take peace, for example. I am not always good at finding peace, but when I do it is amazing. This characteristic will be exponentially better in

Heaven. It will be the best possible peace there is. I mean we will be standing in the presence of the PRINCE OF PEACE. It literally doesn't get any better. So, take these tools seriously and wear them well. It has taken me a very long time to realize I need these pieces of armor all the time. That I should have them shined up and ready to use, not just hidden in a closet somewhere for a bad day. Don't make my mistake and miss out on years of perfecting knowledge of your gear, or of your commander in chief.

One last piece of advice and this one comes to you from both scripture and my kickboxing instructors. Never let your guard down. Get to a point where you are so good at this hand to hand combat stuff, you never give an opportunity for the Devil to get a jab in there. Instead, you are ready and always on guard. I'm not there yet, but long for the day when I am! I can see it now. Me in full tactical gear, strapped in, and throwing some mean right head hooks at the enemy. Boom! Pow! Mount up, warriors. We have armor to don and swords to wield.

11
BELT OF TRUTH

Have you ever had one of those dreams
where you wake up, and you really have no idea if
what you just experienced was real or not? When you
doubt everything, and it takes you a few minutes to
even know where you are? I have these dreams all the
time. It's kind of my thing. I have super weird
dreams. I could fill another book with odd dreams
that I have had and still remember even decades later.
I had another one of those crazy dreams just this
week.

I don't know how I got to this place in the
dream, but I never seem to know how I get there.
Does anyone else know what I'm talking about? Well

somehow, my sister and I end up at a house. We have been taken as slaves to this man, along with many others. It wasn't very pretty. Then we find someone that is going to take us out of there and get us to freedom, only to find out they have lied to us and are instead taking us as slaves for themselves. They had an entire slew of children who were their slaves. Somehow, we managed to escape from their grasp too through a very strange uphill climbing restaurant (why does it always have to be uphill!!). I woke up gasping for air, huffing, and puffing as if I were actually climbing Mount Everest. I had no idea where I was, no clue if I was safe, and was definitely out of breath. It took me a minute, but I finally regained my bearings after repeating to myself, "you are fine. You are at home. You are safe. You are not a slave. There is no one after you." I literally had to speak truth over myself for a while before I actually began to believe it.

Speaking truth over yourself is not just for bad dreams, though, from personal experience it does help you snap out of it. No, speaking truth over our hearts and minds is one of our best defenses we have not only against the enemy but against ourselves. Often times, we are our own worst critic. We actually make the job of destroying our minds easy for the Devil, because we do it for him. Almost willingly at that. We are able to tear ourselves down without ever actually saying a word out loud. We literally don't need anyone else to rip us apart, we do a great job on our own. So how can we use this concept of truth to keep us together? How can we surround ourselves with real facts when the enemy comes knocking? The answer lies in the belt of truth we are equipped with as believers.

The belt of truth is listed in Ephesians as the first piece of armor we are given, which is an important piece of information. It means truth is of the utmost importance to our lives as believers, as a characteristic of our Heavenly Father, and as the piece of armor that holds everything together. Truth is the belt. In Roman times the belt was made of leather or metal, or both. It held the sword and other weapons in place, along with keeping the breastplate secured to the soldier. The same can be said of our own belt of truth, it holds the sword of the spirit (the Word) in place. Thus, linking truth and the Word of God. Meaning, the word of God is the truth.

Without this belt, our armor would fall off and leave us vulnerable. Instead, the belt of truth guards our innermost being in the battle against insecurity and lies from the enemy. It holds us together. It's like a good pair of spanks. Yep, I went there. A good pair of spanks keeps everything in place and leaves a smooth surface for clothing to slip over. It keeps it all tight, and not like the can't breathe in your spanks kind of tight. More like they have it all together, confidently moving around, tight. You ladies know what I mean. You guys, well, just be glad you don't know what I mean.

I don't know about you but speaking truth to myself and actually believing it doesn't come naturally to me. It is something I have to work at, not just saying the words but allowing them to penetrate my heart so that the real work may begin. One way I have found to help speak truth into my life on a daily basis is to start the day with Jesus. I spend about 30 minutes of my morning reading devotionals, reading scriptures, journaling and praying. There are many times this half hour is a slap in the face, and I haven't even finished my cup of coffee yet (well decaf coffee, which to many of you don't think it counts as coffee). But as I wake up, aligning myself with truth, surrounding myself with it, gives me the foundation I need to start the day well. It sets me up to be as successful in speaking truth to myself and others as I possibly can be. Jesus is so faithful to show up in my mornings and confirm the truth.

Another way I wrap myself in truth and belt it on, is I do my best to surround myself with others who will speak truth to me when I am weak. These people are irreplaceable in my life and have changed me forever. They are squad goals to the millionth degree! God is so merciful to have created us as community-oriented people. We need each other and not just sometimes. We need others to help us see the flaws in ourselves, to speak truth over us when we are unable (or unwilling depending on our mood that day), to continue to point us to the only one who can save us, the way, the truth, and the life. Jesus.

Maybe you are someone who needs visual reminders. So, you physically surround yourself with quotes or scriptures about who you are, who has the victory, and the truth of the battle going on around you. Whatever it is that you need to remind you of these vital characteristics, these truth bombs, do it! We cannot do this alone. We need all the help we can get. Trust me! Speaking and living truth all the time is not something we have the tendency to lean towards. In fact, our tendencies are to avoid the truth, especially when it means we are in the wrong and never speak the truth because that can often leave us in the minority.

Look at it from a military perspective. The soldiers operate off of truth. Their missions are planned and executed based off of trusting the intelligence they have received and receiving as the truth. They put their entire faith in this truth and perform orchestrated missions based on this truth. It holds their team together, it aligns their purpose and gives them direction. The same is true of our truth,

THE truth, Jesus. He holds us together. He gives us purpose and direction in life and provides the truth we need in order to make sense of this crazy world we live in. This truth He gives us also helps us with our own mission, reflecting Himself, furthering His kingdom, and fighting off the enemy. Truth is what holds us in place. Surrounding ourselves with the truth of the gospel, the truth of who Christ is, and the truth of who we are in Christ is the belt around our gut. Tighten those belts and let's get to work allowing truth to reign in our lives.

12
BREASTPLATE OF RIGHTEOUSNESS

When looking at the pieces of armor the Lord has given us, it is the breastplate of righteousness that covers our chests, our hearts. Ancient soldiers wore breastplates made of bronze or chain metal secured in place by a belt or straps. It was a critical piece of their armor as they headed into battle. The same is true of our breastplate of righteousness. In Ephesians, Paul uses the imagery of armor as a way to describe the characteristics God is giving to His children. In this case, the breastplate is the salvation offered to us through Jesus Christ. The breastplate protects us from evil if we are in Christ. He has given us His breastplate to wear, to guard us against the enemy.

Scriptures spend a good amount of space telling us to protect our most vital organ, to guard our hearts. Protecting my heart is not something I would claim to have done well in my life. When I look back, I feel as though I often gave my heart to people who didn't deserve it or worn it on my sleeve where it was incredibly vulnerable. While neither of those things is exactly bad in themselves, they can leave a heart bruised, maybe even broken. But also, it leaves the most vital organ in my being to be open to the enemy when that is not what God intended for me.

It took me a long time to work on guarding my heart. Mostly because when I was growing up no one really taught us how to guard our hearts. They just told us we needed to do it. So, for me, guarding my heart tended to feel like I was being disingenuous or fake around people. I hated that feeling. I didn't like feeling as if I have to hide part of myself in an effort to protect myself. I was fine with the idea of protecting myself but didn't want it to have to come at the cost of not being me in situations or around certain people. Again, there wasn't a lot of curriculum around how to actually guard one's heart. It wasn't until much later in life, and after many mistakes, that I learned what guarding my heart actually meant. And even in knowing what it means, I'm not sure I am that good at the action yet. Let me give you a silly (but very personal) example.

Growing up I never really felt pretty. I was confident and thought I was smart, sometimes funny, occasionally talented in different things, but never actually pretty. I'm not saying I didn't like how I looked, I just would have never put myself in the beautiful category. When someone gave me a compliment about my looks, I would say something like "oh it's the new makeup I have on" or "this new shampoo really does make my hair look good." I never really let the compliment be directed at me personally, but at things infused with products. Yes, the products were beautiful, but I just wasn't. Now before you go crazy on me, as a female, I think every woman in the world feels this way about something. It may be not being pretty, it may be not being smart or athletic, or they don't think they are talented in comparison to other people. We are always not good enough for something. (Spoiler Alert: We are human. If we were good enough, we wouldn't have needed a Savior in the first place. Just throwing that fact in here to give some perspective.) I guarded myself so much from what other people saw me as, especially when it came to physical appearance, that I literally couldn't accept someone giving me a compliment. To this day, I'm still not sure there are many people in the world who could call me beautiful, and I believe them. I have spent so many years "guarding" myself from others in the area, that even now I have a hard time adjusting and trusting the words they are trying to give me as encouragement, praise, or admiration. It stinks, but it's the truth.

I use this story as an example to show you what guarding yourself shouldn't look like. I was reading a devotional on Lent today from a book called 40 days of Decrease by Alicia Britt Chole. I'm about a third of the way through the 40 days and today's reflection so closely aligns with this concept of being on guard. Chole wrote, "Self-protection is not always unhealthy. For instance, when we brace ourselves for an impending car accident or run when chased by an angry animal, we are instinctively self-protecting our physical bodies... Self-protection in these examples is a response to danger: we self-protect when we do not feel safe. Therefore, when we spiritually self-protect, is it because we do not feel safe with God?" Ouch. Reread that last question again. Do we not feel safe with God? I don't know about you, but that question stopped me for a good 10 minutes this morning. I mean, do I not feel safe with God? Is that why I guard things, spiritually and personally? Because I don't feel protected? The answer to all of these questions at the deepest levels of my heart is yes. At the end of the day, I am a scared girl doing her best to be brave and to protect myself from harm, even possible harm from a Heavenly Father I know I will disappoint. Like, it is guaranteed I will mess it up. Ugh. I hate messing up. And yet, He knows I will and loves me anyway.

So why do I feel so insecure? So unsafe? Because somewhere along the way I thought guarding my heart meant not letting others into the depths of who I am, including God. Writing that sentence brings me to tears both of sadness and joy. Sadness because I know how many years I have wasted not letting God have every part of my heart and accepting the compliments He was speaking over me as His most prized daughter and co-heiress with Jesus. And joy because God never stopped chiseling away at the brick walls I built around myself in an effort to guard my heart against invasion, whether it be invaded by human or the Divine. He never gave up on me, nor did He ever stop wanting to know the real me. And in His pursuit, I learned He is the only one who can truly guard my heart and be my Protector. I must trust Him with His wisdom, His perspective and His love for me that He has the best in mind and will act accordingly. Guarding my heart had very little to do with me, and everything to do with releasing that part of me to the one who created it in the first place. Thus, God lovingly serves as my breastplate.

Now there is another important word describing this breastplate that we haven't talked about yet. It is that big, amazing word- righteousness. This really long, Christianese word is what God is guarding us with, so maybe we should figure out what it is. When you look up the word righteousness, the definition you should see is something along the lines of meaning the quality of being morally right or justifiable. How I was taught to remember what righteousness means is to think right-ness, you are made right or reconciled with something. Justified. Being justified implies that we have somehow been judged and found on the pleasing side of that judgment. And hallelujah friends, that statement could not be truer! We have been made right with God, found pleasing in His judgment of our lives, not because of anything we have done, but because of what guards us. And what is it that guards us again? The breastplate of righteousness, the salvation that guards us, Jesus Christ himself.

That's right. This breastplate of righteousness we are to strap on for battle is none other than Jesus himself living in us. The Salvation of the world guarding his brothers and sisters as we head to battle and protecting our hearts from the invasion of the enemy. This is our armor. I am telling you, friends, there is nothing stronger out there to keep us safe. There is no alarm system, self-defense class, or federal law that will be able to protect us from the schemes of the Devil. Only Jesus can do that. He is the only one who can withstand the blows heading for your heart. And we are called to put on this breastplate daily. We have to be the ones to make the decision that allows Jesus the place he needs in our lives in order to protect us. It is a daily task and lifelong action required to allow the Savior to continue His job of saving you. But it is a worthy pursuit, my friend.

13
SHOES OF PEACE

I like shoes. Clearly, I like shoes. I mean I wrote a book called *Sweatpants & Stilettos*. I wouldn't say that I am in love with shoes or that I have a need to always have a new pair, but I do appreciate a good pair of stylish shoes. Comfort is sometimes negotiable. But what I have discovered about the difference between shoes I love and shoes I don't, is not just how they look, but also how they feel. Number 1 question being, can I walk in them? And then passed that, how do I feel in them? Am I confident in them, do I feel shaky, are they stable enough? Usually, if I feel good, feel confident, and feel stable the shoes are going in the basket. (Well and if I am in need. I mean, I'm on a budget!) So, the deciding factor isn't really always about how they look on me, but rather do they give me a firm foundation to stand on.

When I think about the shoes of peace, my mind automatically associates this same feeling with how I am supposed to be wearing this piece of armor. Can I walk in them? How do I feel in them? Am I confident? Are they stable? Do they provide me with a strong foundation on which to move? Applying these questions to the regular shoe buying process is easy for me. The second I start applying them to shoes of peace, it is nothing short of convicting. Because if I'm being completely honest (which apparently, I don't know another way to write a book, so you know I'm being honest), the answer to most of these questions is I don't know. Maybe yes, maybe no. Or goodness I hope so! I know I can't be the only one who sometimes thinks peace seems like an elusive carrot forever being bated in front of me but out of reach. Am I? If you were here, I would hope to hear a few amens. Since you aren't, I will just imagine a stadium full of confirmation. Ok? Thanks!

With these questions in mind, if I am meant to wear shoes of peace, this first thing I ask myself is "can I walk in them?." This is a rough place to start, but we have to start somewhere. Can I walk in shoes of peace? Am I able to stand firm in peace regardless of what is going on around me? Can I walk in a peace that surpasses my own understanding of the situation? Can I walk in peace no matter what? AHHHH I DON'T KNOW! Well, at least that is what I know the Devil is telling me. He's wanting me to doubt my strength in the Lord. But aside from the devil's scheming, do I actually believe peace is even possible for me to walk in? Friends, until a couple of months ago I would have told you for my type A personality, peace was a nice idea but not something I ever thought possible for myself. It is not because I didn't think the Lord could bring me peace, I knew He could and would. It was that I doubted I would know what to do with it when it came and would instead fill my life with the exact opposite of peace.

Let me explain a little bit here why I say this. I am SUPER type A. I like plans. I like staying busy. I like knowing what my day is going to look like and I do not typically enjoy surprises or interruptions. I also enjoy having a full calendar. I think I'm pretty awful at being still, enjoying the moment, and taking care of myself with periods of rest. So, when I say I didn't think peace was possible for me, what I mean is, every other time in my life where I was given the time, space and capacity to embrace peace I chose to fill it with some other activity. I chose to invite plans and chaos, and stress in rather than be vulnerable and let peace reign in my life. Peace felt like a weakness to me. And I, like a brave warrior, was above weakness. Arrogant, right?

Then I entered into a season where everything in my life is in question. Where I will work, what my job will be, where I will live, what my relationships will look like, what my ministry and church life will change too, what my priorities in money will reflect. Just about every area of my life is on the table right now. And I am just hanging out waiting for God to provide the answers. And normal Rachel, the super type A one I have known for the last 30 years of my life, would be FREAKING OUT right now. I would be making contingency plans for each scenario of all of the questions I listed above and then have back up plans for those contingencies. I would be stressed. My mind would constantly run on overdrive, and I would be running myself into the ground. I know this because this is how I reacted just last year in another life-altering season. And of course, I'm going to share it with you, because that's what I do. Share my stupid moments, so hopefully, you have less of them, or maybe just different ones!

Whelp, here's what happened. Ugh. I don't even want to type this paragraph because it was so awful and so opposite of peace. But the Lord has called me to live a brave life, and here it goes. Last summer I worked hard to complete the first three chapters of my dissertation. I had a timeline, and I stuck to it. I finished before the new semester was going to start in August and I was ready to go. The chair of my committee was not. He had other things for me to do before he felt I was ready to present my proposal. That was strike one against peaceful Rachel. I had worked so hard, and now there was even more delay. But I sucked it up and kept going, knowing it would get worked out eventually. September came along, and I got some awful news at work. Like the kick in the gut kind of bad news. It was the kind where you question if what you are doing is worth it and if you are making a difference at all.

I spent the better part of the next six weeks questioning my entire professional life. Strike two. October was the real kick in the teeth when I received, out of the blue, that the relationship I had with a close friend of mine was going to have to drastically change. For this situation, I cried. For weeks I cried. Strike three. And while all of this destruction was happening around me, I still had the chapters for my dissertation to complete and a presentation to prepare. Strike four. AND THEN, on top of everything else I got an ulcer. Yep, the physical manifestation of stress (aka anti-peace) found its way into my body. Strike five.

I wish I could tell you I handled each of those blows with grace and peace at the center of my character, but it just wasn't. Obviously, it wasn't. I mean I had an ulcer for goodness sakes! Nothing about my spirit, my soul, or my body was at peace. I was constantly trying to plan for the future that I had no idea how I was going to be able to handle. Or attempting to pull myself together enough to get through the packed schedule I had in front of me, finish tasks that had timelines, and still brush my teeth. Peace wasn't even on my radar. Not that the Lord wouldn't have provided it, but I didn't ask for it. I asked to survive. I asked for the pain to go away. I didn't ask for peace. I asked for a release from my situations. Which is still a valid prayer. Jesus did the same in the garden before his journey to the cross, but he continued to on the path in front of him regardless. I wasn't going to continue on the path. I didn't care if the Lord was going to release me from my situations or not, I couldn't live this way. It was terrible. Looking back, how could a life without peace be anything but difficult?

Something in me broke from that experience. The Lord has torn me down to my studs and sought to rebuild me on a foundation of peace. And that is the only reason I am able to talk about peace as something that is possible regardless of the decisions that need to be made, the closure that you desire to have, or the mountains that seem immovable. The six months ago Rachel would be dying right now if she saw how many big questions I have unanswered in so many areas of my life right now. I don't even know if she would be standing. But God... Ahhhh just those two words make me want to close my eyes and exhale. But God, rich in mercy and love for me, picked me out of that pit of despair and set me on a foundation of peace. I literally have NO IDEA what He is up to, or what is to come for me. And for the first time in my entire life, I am 100% ok not having a plan or an idea of a plan. That is INSANE. I still can't believe I am able to say those words, let alone actually mean them.

What I have learned about peace in the last few months is peace is not a vulnerability, it is a strength. It is like the vibranium steel of metals. Which for those non-Marvel people out there (I'm lovingly rolling my eyes at you), is the metal that Captain America's shield is made out of. It is fictionally, the strongest metal in the world and completely indestructible. This is the same as the peace God provides for us. It doesn't make us weak, it actually makes us indestructible. A person at peace cannot be moved. They cannot be shaken.

Peace is also not just a feeling, it is an act of faith. I thought if I had peace then I would just feel better. I would feel happy. I would be carefree. But it is not just about feeling at peace. I would venture to guess there are very few moments in anyone's life that they feel completely at peace. It just is not physically possible with so many distractions to be at peace without help or intervention of some kind. Rather, peace is an action. It requires us to continue releasing our worries, questions, doubts, and concerns to the Prince. Giving Him back His throne and trusting He will do what He says He will do: provide and protect.

I strongly believe peace comes when we begin

to remove obstacles from our life, even seemingly good obstacles, that keep us from living out the gospel. In Ephesians, Paul doesn't just describe the shoes as peace, but as shoes that are to be used to prepare us to bring the gospel of peace. Knowing what peace is (and what it is not) should help us be ready to bring about the gospel of it. Why? Because the soul-giving peace we have is only available through Jesus Christ. He is the gospel. And we have to be ready to share that truth, that gospel of peace, with everyone. So then, not only are we to be ready to proclaim the gospel itself but also to help others understand the inner peace we have as believers. A victory of any kind in this battle is not possible without Jesus and inner peace. In order to get to the finish line, we have to have confidence that God will get us there because we already know we won't make it on our own. Therefore, we need something that will snuff out the anxious thoughts, the crippling fear, and the nagging worry. And that is where peace flourishes if you let it.

Understanding more about how peace works,

I see why Paul partners it with shoes. Shoes are ESSENTIAL to the equipment of a warrior. I would hate to go into battle with nothing protecting my feet. I would be awful in battle. Forget battle! I can't even walk without shoes down the sidewalk of my apartment complex without complaining. My feet are that sensitive. How are we supposed to stand or even walk into battle without a strong foundation on which to stand? Paul knew we had to be brave, confident, and on stable ground to be well equipped. And he knew the gospel of peace was the foundation on which warriors were always meant to stand.

14
SHIELD OF FAITH

I have seen some hard days in the last two months. Days where I was crying more hours of the day than not. It's a terrible feeling. It's demotivating and crippling. For me, it holds me hostage. Even if I didn't want to be crying or sad, still it is there. It is always in those moments where I really have to sit and constantly remind myself that the Lord is in this too. He has to be. He isn't a god that is only there for good things. He is there for ALL the things. And ALL the things mean, good AND bad. So how do I get to a point where I can accept that the bad things are just as important to God as the good things? How do I let myself even begin to be ok with the bad things in the first place? Faith.

One word. It sounds incredibly easy, but it is probably one of the most difficult things I have tried to cultivate in my life. Faith is the tool the Lord gives us to have hope when we don't understand. It is a guard of our hearts and minds. It is our shield just as it says it is in Ephesians, the shield of faith. It is a defensive piece of equipment the Lord has graciously given to us to help us fight the battle we are in. And crazy enough, faith is not stagnant. It can be increased! That should be such good news to us as believers. The amount of faith we start with does not have to be the amount of faith we end up with. It can grow. And in my experience, it must grow. It must be stretched and tested in order for us to have it become fully ours and fully what the Lord has planned for us.

Have you ever asked for your faith to be increased? I used to approach this prayer like praying for patience. I never pray for patience because I'm afraid God will then give me a circumstance through which to learn patience. And man, I hope I don't have any more lessons in patience. (P.S. I know that's impractical. I will continue to have a MILLION lessons in patience throughout the rest of my life. I will need every single one of them. But can't a girl hope for a few less? I mean can I get an Amen??) So just like I'm not always excited about a lesson in patience, I haven't really approached increasing my faith with a positive attitude. I'm sure that sounds incredibly un-Christian of me, but I'm just being honest. Living a faith-filled life is HARD, and I'm a wimp sometimes. I don't want to have to be strong all the time or keep learning lessons. It can be exhausting. And that is exactly where the Lord steps in. He takes my rebellious and tainted human heart and fills it with faith, love, patience, joy, and a multitude of other fruits to keep me growing.

I finally overcame my fear and asked the Lord to increase my faith. To draw me closer to Him. To remove anything that would stand in the way of my relationship with Him and return me to His loving presence. I asked, and He is responding. And it is painful. Needed and will be beautiful, but painful. Remember at the beginning of this chapter how I said

I was constantly crying? That's because the Lord has been using the last couple of months to remove things in my life that have been certainties, unshakable staples in my life that I have used to identify who I am, used to fill my time. They aren't bad things, but they are things I never would've questioned before. And now here I am trying my absolute best to increase my faith, believe the Lord knows what He is doing, and let Him prune away any identifier that isn't Him. And it is so dang painful.

You see, I have clung to my title at work or my position volunteering, or even the friendships I have surrounded myself with in life. All good things in and of themselves. But when they are in the way of where Jesus wants you to be, or they are keeping you so comfortable you don't want to go where He is leading, then He will remove them. He will remove all barriers that keep you from the good that He has for you and from being solely His. He is a jealous God. We are His precious, prized possession and He does not share His children with other things, even if they are seemingly good. He has such amazing plans for us that He will do everything He can to make sure that is where we end up. Through tears of sadness or of joy, He will take you there.

And friend, I hope you aren't as stubborn as I am. I hope you are able to let things go easily and let Him get to work. Me? I've been stubborn. The idea of going somewhere new freaks me out. Literally, I'm so frightened it makes me want to throw up. Not because I don't trust that He knows what He is doing, but what if I mess it up? What if it is even more painful? Or what if it is far better than I could ever imagine? Guys. I'm so messed up. Why are our human hearts so fickle? Why can't I just be happy that the Lord is at work in my life, painful or not? Because I'm dumb. Are you dumb too? If you are, welcome to the club of imperfect humans and people who mess up all the time. Nice to meet you!

Here's what I know so far, increasing faith is a necessary step in my growth for me to be able to move forward. My favorite C.S. Lewis quote is "There are far, far better things ahead than any we leave behind." It is on my alarm when I wake up in the morning. I have a beautiful print of it from one of my students framed on my wall in my room. I even have it written on a post-it note stuck to my computer at the office. Better things ahead than any we leave behind. That implies there will be all kinds of things that we will be required to leave behind though. And some of them may be good things. It also means there is so much more ahead for us, better things if we would only go. And we get there through increasing our faith, stepping out in courage, and trusting that God knows what He is doing even when we don't understand or see it.

You see, He is always privy to the bigger picture. I am not. Which is probably a good thing. I would freak out, start over thinking, and over planning and mess it all up on day one. No, He slowly shows me a piece at a time. I wish I could tell you He has shown me the next piece to direct me in this current pruning process, but He hasn't. The most encouraging word He has given me are two thoughts from two different verses. One from Psalms 31:24, "Be strong and courageous all you who put your hope in the Lord." My hope in the Lord is all I have right now to get me through the craziness I currently find myself in. The second is from Esther 4: 14, "Perhaps you were created for such a time as this." This verse gets me every time. Created for a time of pain you may ask? Yes. Pain brings about change, and the Lord is very clearly pointing me in the direction of change. These two verses embolden me to believe the Lord knows what He is doing, that I was created with a specific purpose, and that He will grant me the courage to walk forward confidently. I'm called to be a Wonder Woman of faith. Brave and purpose-filled. All of which will require increasing my faith. Using it has a shield. Yielding it one day at a time.

15
HELMET OF SALVATION

In conjunction with guarding our hearts, the Bible repeatedly reminds us of how we must also guard our minds. Do you ever stop to wonder why those two things are so important? Why the heart and mind? Biologically speaking they are two vital organs which must function properly in order for us to stay alive. Emotionally both play a part in how we make decisions and how we respond to situations we find ourselves in. Spiritually speaking, they are gateways into the most intimate parts of our bodies and souls. So, it should be no surprise to me that Paul associates the helmet, the piece of armor responsible for protecting the head and brain, with salvation.

What, then, is salvation? I am so glad you asked! To put it as simply as a possible salvation, for Christians, is deliverance from sin and its consequences. This deliverance can only happen through faith in Christ and what He has done for us on the cross. Once someone has received salvation for the first time, they are part of the family! It is so amazing. But the thing we sometimes forget is that salvation doesn't just happen to us that one day and it's done. No, salvation is something we have to repeatedly speak over ourselves, over our minds in an effort to reorient ourselves when we've wandered away. And we will wander. We are dumb sheep remember. We get ourselves in trouble, we get lost, we even don't know when to stop. Just like sheep, we need someone there to remind us of the direction to go, the truth of who we belong to and where our identity lies. We need to speak salvation to ourselves constantly.

So, when do we speak this salvation over our minds? All the time! But to be a bit more specific, let me give you a few examples from my own life. Here's

an example from my day today. Today was a normal
Sunday for me. I got up, went to kickboxing, ran
some errands and was on my way to a leadership
meeting with my ministry team. This is normal for me
because I go to church on Saturday evenings. The
ministry team doesn't meet every week, maybe more
like twice a semester to plan our events and make sure
everyone knows what is coming up. So that part was
also not exactly normal but planned and on the
calendar. I get to the church a little early to the
meeting, and a message comes in saying it is canceled
due to people not being able to attend. My initial
response was not joyful. I had literally just gotten
there after driving for 20 minutes, and now I had
about 2 hours until the ministry evening actually
started. I was frustrated and annoyed. I really dislike
when people cancel meetings without notice,
especially after I've made the effort to get there on
time. I felt like I had been disrespected. I drove home
in a bad mood the whole way, with no desire to
return in a couple of hours to do ministry. Sadly, I
actually considered not going at all. Thankfully my
wiser brain kicked in and realized not going doesn't

help anything.

After a few minutes at home and a good cup of tea, I calmed down. I stopped to thank God for a few extra hours to get things done before work tomorrow, and then enjoyed just sitting which is something I don't get to do very often. I prayed and asked a friend of mine to pray that my attitude would improve before I headed back out to minister to my middle schoolers. Nothing is worse than heading into a ministry setting and having a bad attitude. By the time I got there I was better and not because of anything in me, but because of salvation. The salvation I had to speak over myself that ministry was not about me. That plans change, and nothing in the act of changing schedules was meant as a personal attack. That sometimes things just happen or don't happen as it didn't in this instance. None of those things have anything to do with me, my identity, or my value. And that is what speaking salvation over myself looked like today. Reminding myself that nothing in this world, good or bad, will change my final destination, my purpose for pursuing Christ or my worth.

This example may sound small, but how often are you there? How often do things change and the bad attitude comes to life, and then you find yourself in a downward spiral? Maybe that spiral is only a few minutes, maybe it's your day that is ruined. Or maybe it has evolved into a lifetime of negativity and loss of who you really are in Christ. Which is a delivered soul! You are set free from things that try to weigh us down, even dumb thinks like a bad attitude or things not going our way. There are much bigger examples throughout my life where I questioned who I was, why I was there, or where my worth came from. MANY TIMES these questions have plagued my mind. And they aren't bad questions to ask. In fact, they can often be healthy. As long as you are using those moments to speak salvation over your mind, then it is healthy. But mind games are some of the Devil's favorite tactics, and he is VERY good at what he does.

You remember the story of Lazarus dying. In John 11, Jesus hears of his dear friend, Lazarus, being sick in a town not far from where He is. Instead of going straight to His friend, Jesus delays. He waits. Two whole days go by before He journeys to the next city over to meet up with Lazarus and his family, Mary and Martha. In those two days, Lazarus dies. His body has already been wrapped and put in the grave. The mourners are there to weep with Mary and Martha, and that is when Jesus decided to show up. I don't know about you, but at first glance, I would be upset.

Jesus missed everything. He could have come sooner; healed Lazarus and this whole thing would have been a party. Instead, they had mourners. There were tears and sadness, not dancing and joy. Jesus could have fixed this sooner! And everyone there knew He could have healed His friend. That's the human way of looking at this situation. Thankfully, God looks at things a little differently than we do. He sees a much bigger picture, as did His son, Jesus. No Jesus waited, cried with His friends and then said enough. Then He prayed to His Heavenly Father and then called Lazarus to come out of the grave, and he did. He was raised from the dead. And do you know why? Verse 40 tells us. Jesus says raising Lazarus from the grave was not for His benefit, but for God's and for the people that were gathered there. Verse 40 says, "did I not tell you that if you believed you would see the glory of God?". Lazarus died so that others could see the glory of God. I don't know about you, but when bad situations happen, it isn't always my first instinct to believe it is for the glory of God. In fact, sometimes it is downright difficult to understand how God could use destructive or painful things for His glory. But just because it is difficult to see, doesn't make it any less true. God always uses our circumstances to show us His glory.

So how do we get from seeing it as a painful situation to an opportunity for glory? Salvation. Salvation steps in to remind us of the gift we have been given, the freedom that comes with that gift, and the things we have been rescued from. It reminds us that at the end of the day, eternity is all that matters. The rest of this stuff will fall and fade, but the worst possible thing, the penalty of death for our sins, has already been paid for us. We have complete confidence our future is secure. And that is something worth repeating over and over and over again. To ourselves, to our spouses, our families, our friends, our leaders, our students, our guests, our neighbors, and our enemies. The act of receiving salvation is one time and forever, but the act of living salvation is a lifetime learning process. It is a constant refreshing of the mind and reorienting of the spirit. And the best north star we have to fix our minds on is what our sweet Jesus has done for us, granted us a free gift of salvation. Once we get it, wear the helmet of salvation well and wear it often for it is one of our greatest defenses.

16
SWORD OF THE SPIRIT

It sits in the top drawer of my nightstand, where I can find it easily through sleep eyes, or tear-filled eyes. It has been with me for almost two decades even though the version isn't my favorite anymore. It is worn, ripped, discolored, and creased. It has seen me through glorious days and dark nights. It has brought me wisdom, encouragement, hope, and truth. It is one of my most valued possessions. It is my copy of the Bible, the living word of God, the sword of the Spirit.

Did you notice in the armor listed in Ephesians, there is only one weapon? Paul gives us only one thing to defend ourselves with, everything else is protection. The sword is for defense. I find this fact fascinating, and maybe you don't, but you can just play along for now. With everything the Lord equips us with, the one weapon He allows us to have is His word. The thing to beat off the enemy, the linchpin of the operation, the final blow, are all found in the words He wrote to us. We've all heard the saying, the pen is mightier than the sword. Well, in this case, the pen, the words are written in the Bible, are in fact the sword we have been given. Take that, colloquialisms!

But in all seriousness, the Bible is a phenomenal gift God has given to us, and He was specific in describing it as a sword. Why do you think that is? Scripture wasn't described as a sword only in Ephesians. Actually, it shows up again in Hebrews where the author describes the Bible, "For the word of God is living and powerful, and sharper than any two-edged sword, piercing even to the division of soul and spirit, and of joints and marrow, and is a discerner of the thoughts and intents of the heart.

And there is no creature hidden from His sight, but all things are naked and open to the eyes of Him to whom we must give account" (Hebrews 4:12-13). You see that? The word of God is living, powerful, and sharp. If it is living, it moves and understands life. If it is powerful, it has strength behind the blows it makes. If it is sharp, it has the ability to pierce the opponent deeply. That sounds like a decent weapon to me.

Not only is the sword of the Spirit meant as a weapon for us, but also as a defensive mechanism. It is valuable in deflecting attacks from the enemy. Remember when Jesus was in the wilderness for 40 days (in Matthew 4), He was using that time to fast and draw near to His Father. He had been without food or water for 40 days, and He was physically weak. Which is of course when Satan decides to show up and tempted Jesus. And what does Jesus say to Satan and his advances? Jesus quotes scriptures to not only make His point but also to defend Himself against the enemy. If Jesus needed to use His sword, the Word, to fight off Satan, you can bet we do too!

But how do we do that? How do we use scripture to defend ourselves and keep us on what is true? The easy answer is by taking care of our weapons and sharpening our swords.

In the military, soldiers are taught to take special care of their weapons. Not only are they taught how to use them, but how to clean them, disassemble, reassemble, and how to store their weapons properly. In the first week of basic training, soldiers aren't even allowed to shoot their weapon. They just learn about it and get comfortable carrying it with them wherever they go. So comfortable with the gun, they are told to give it a name. They spend hours working to understand every aspect of their weapon, how to take it apart, how to clean it, what it feels like loaded and unloaded. They learn how to check the weapon safely for when something isn't working properly, and it is drilled into their heads. After they are comfortable with their weapons, they spend two or three days on the range, shooting all day under any circumstance. This piece of metal is the most important system they have as a solder. It is their lifeline.

If soldiers spend so much time and energy understanding and besting their physical weapons, how much more do we need to know and understand our spiritual weapons? I would love to say that understanding scripture and knowing in your time of need is easy, but it's not. It's not easy, because it takes work. It takes time. And it takes a willingness to keep at it, over and over again. That's the funny and amazing thing about reading the "living" word of God. I can read the same verse every day for a week, and there will be something different I see in it or hear from God in it. It is a living weapon. It adapts to our needs, or what the Lord is helping us to understand better. I'm not saying the words on the page change. No, the Word of God is true and 100% correct as it is. What I am saying, is that my perspective and understanding change as circumstances come into my life, as I mature, and I gain more information.

We learn scriptures by memorizing it. Jesus had the Old Testament down for exactly that moment when Satan would come taunting Him. He KNEW them so well. And we can too. It is sitting there waiting for you to open the cover and start somewhere. The scriptures I have memorized are usually the ones I learned as a kid going through bible drill. But man, sometimes I wish there was Bible drill for adults! You had to know all the books of the Bible, be able to locate them in the physical book itself, memorize scriptures, and then be able to locate passages all in 10 seconds! If more adults knew how to do that, what kind of difference would that bring to our ministries? It shows a level of importance, doesn't it? We place knowing the Bible as such a high priority that we can quote it in 10 seconds. I don't know about you, but there are tons of things I can quote in 10 seconds. Most of them are Disney songs or movie quotes. I can quote some scriptures too, the ones that have been with me for decades. But there are people I know that scripture just flows from. They have studied it, memorized it, and equipped themselves with it. I don't know their motive for seeking that level of understanding, but regardless the Lord will use it for His glory. It can't be a bad thing to have more people running around this chaotic globe who can quote scriptures!

We also learn more about the Bible by reading it. I mean really reading it. Not the reading we do in school, skimming, but actually reading. I realized a while ago this is something I was never taught. I am an academic at heart, so knowing how to study is one thing I think I do a decent job at. But I didn't want to approach the Bible like a textbook, or a class required reading source. I wanted it to be more personal, more in-depth, and meaningful. I wanted it to stick with me, not just enlighten me for the moment and then move on. So last summer I read a book with my small group on how to study the bible by Jen Wilkin. It was a great reference to help me learn how best to read the bible and study it. Jen broke down some of the best methods and techniques for studying the Bible on an impactful level. I would gladly encourage you to pick up a copy of her book, Women of the Word: How to Study the Bible with Both Our Hearts and Our Minds.

Another way to sharpen our swords is to use

them as frequently as possible. Things stick with repetition. The Word is meant to be our guiding post of wisdom, the spirit that helps us discern truth and good from evil. How will we ever get to a level of proficiency with the scriptures if we do not put it into regular use? Roman soldiers trained extensively with wooden swords before they were given the opportunity to train with real blades. It was not just the weight they were getting used to, but how to move with this weapon, how to defend against advances, and how to build endurance using the sword in battle. A sword is not a lightweight weapon, and the Bible isn't either. It is a weighty text, filled with every type of literary structure. It isn't just a recording of history, or simply an elaborate story. It is guidance and wisdom, history and poetry, symbolism and metaphors, life advice and learning examples. And it is all packed into 66 books breathed by God Himself. It is our job as believers to know this book. It is our weapon against the enemy and the love letter from our Heavenly Father.

So, I guess the real question is, do you want to

be skilled in the use of your sword? As a soldier in a constant battle, what level of comfort do you want to have with the weapon you are equipped with? Do you desire to have a high level of skill with this tool? How valuable is it to you? The answer should be yes you want to have a high level of skill with this sword. I ask these questions because they are something I ask myself all the time. Or even more personally, I ask "is reading the word, spending time with God more valuable to you than watching TV right now?" That is really a hard question. Of course, we want to know the Word, but do we want to know it more than we want to veg out on the couch? Or more than hitting the snooze button 3 times in the morning? That last one is the one I struggle with the most. But I keep at it. I continue to ask myself hard questions to put it into perspective just how important knowing the Bible is. Not just for me, but others as well. Just as Proverbs 27:17 says, "As iron sharpens iron, so one person sharpens another." Someone who is wholeheartedly working to understand more of the Bible and the God who wrote it will sharpen and encourage others around them to do the same. We are in this together, and we are sharpening one another as we learn to sharpen and use our swords daily.

17
BATTLE BUDDIES

For many years, I have had the privilege of
doing life with a few other females who I consider to
be my family. They have seen me at my worst, at my
best, and everything in between. They know all there
is to know about me. The inside, outside, upside,
downside (Happy all the time!! Anyone else start
singing that song? No? Just me? Ok cool. Moving
on). They have prayed with me, cried with me,
laughed with me, and just sat silently with me when
there was nothing left to say. They are the support
system of champions, and I am thankful to call each
one of them a sister in Christ and a friend for a
lifetime. With this badge of honor, however, comes

great responsibility. See I am not one of those people who stay the same. Ever. I am constantly trying to improve something. Trying to be more prayerful, trying to be more chill, less stressed out, more relaxed, less controlling, more trusting, less cynical. So if you are going to be my friend for life, you are going to help me change. Period. It's in the job description.

Now, these ladies didn't know that when they met me. They saw me as a funny, encouraging, loving, smart, handy, loyal… I'll stop there… friend to have around. They saw another person to hang out with, talk to, and laugh with. But from there we grew into something else. We grew into this sisterhood of faith, this bond of betterment, this group of accountability. We became battle buddies.

In the military, a battle buddy is a person that never leaves your side. Quite literally. They are with you everywhere at every moment every day. You are never alone. Talk about knowing everything about a person? They know your movements, begin to recognize how you think, how you operate. They start to know your life, your family, your faults, your strengths, your favorites, your pet peeves. They actually know everything there is to know about you. There are no secrets. You withhold nothing from them because in the crux of any given moment it could be life or death. They are building in you the trust that it takes to say, "I will follow you anywhere." Wow. I'm not saying that to sound dramatic, but to emphasize to you just how important this individual is to a soldier. I don't know about you, but I'm not sure I've met anyone that trusts me enough to go into battle with me. Literal battle, dance battle, or even the battle of the sexes game. I mean what a bond between two. What a stronghold of trust.

This is the prime picture of accountability. It is for you to have another person, usually on the same level as you if not a little higher, to do life with. To have someone that knows your every move, every weakness, every hang-up, every wound. They know your scars, your fears, your triumphs, and your tears. This is why as believers we are encouraged to do life with other believers, in a community and accountable to one another. Because this life is hard enough to try and do it by ourselves, let alone try and get anything right. We need one another. We were designed to need one another. And yet, what do we do? We turn away thinking we can do it all on our own, kicking and screaming all the way to the end of ourselves.

Instead, I believe the Lord has called us to do life together. As scriptures tell us over and over again, we are meant to live in community. It sharpens us (Proverbs 27:17), spurs us (Hebrews 10:24-25), encourages us (Romans 15:5), to name a few. Here is what this looks like to me, in my personal life. I have a set group of women I meet with on a regular basis. They are in the same age range. I have met with them for more than 5 years. The group number and members ebb and flow, but there have been two of us that have remained constant. She is my accountability partner. Before life got crazy and I went back to school, we would meet every Saturday morning at 8 am in a local Starbucks, because who has better things to do at 8 am on a Saturday morning right?? Ha. We would meet for an hour and a half and discuss everything. Our week, what the Lord has been doing in our lives, what He has shown us in our quiet times, finances, food issues, workout plans, relationships, struggles, victories, joyful moments, and tearful hours. We would discuss personal goals we wanted to achieve in a certain timeframe, and each week we had to provide an update to where we were on those goals, how we were doing, what the progress or regression had been. We literally did life together. We had no secrets, no judgments, no prejudice, and lots of prayers.

Even now with my life insane, I still meet with this accountability partner of mine. Now it is more of an every other week kind of arrangement to accommodate my study/work/life/sanity schedule. But the vigor and depth of what we discuss, how we interact with one another, and the meaningful, often brutally honest conversations we have, are still just as vital to my personal, spiritual, mental, emotional, and physical growth as most things I have done this side of Heaven.

Now do I think I have the handle on this whole accountability thing? No. Is it one of the easiest things I have ever done? Heck no. It is actually one of the most difficult because of the level of vulnerability you must show to one another. I mean why would you WANT to tell someone else your deepest secrets, your biggest, blackest sins, your torturous temptations? Who does that? We do. I do. You should. Because as crazy as it sounds, having someone else there with you, having your battle buddy by your side 24/7 is one of the most freeing feelings in the world. You aren't alone. You have someone there, in this same crazy stage of life as you, telling you to take just one more step, walk one more mile, take one more shot, study one more hour, read one more chapter, pray one more time, sing one more song, let go one more time. Just typing those sentences makes me stop and take a deep breath, blow it out, and be incredibly thankful for this battle buddy of mine. For her valor, her honesty, her strength, character, faith, prayers, friendship, and deep love that she has for her Savior.

Accountability is there so that when you are standing in your faith, you are able to stand stronger with someone by your side. You are able to fight the good fight because you have fellow soldiers alongside you, beating down the enemy next to you, and claiming victory with you. They are there to remind you how we are called to trust the Lord, fight against the darkness that is at work in this world dragging us down, and to remind you to just keep at it. That is doing life together. That is what entering into battle together looks like. That is the value of a true battle buddy.

Part Three:

Fighting the Good Fight

18
MISSING THE MARK (FAILURES)

Have you ever failed? Like really messed up in a big way with there was no potential way of fixing it? Have you experienced that gut-wrenching feeling of knowing you have lost respect in someone's eyes or lost love because of something you didn't do? No need to tell me, I already know you have. You've failed. BIG TIME. The reason I know this, is because I have failed before in big ways. And it wasn't a great feeling, but you know me by now and you know I'm going to share my huge blunder with you. I mean if I can't share my biggest life screw ups with friends, who can I share them with? So here it goes.

If you didn't already know, I am in the final stages of my dissertation as I write this book. Yes, I'm writing a book while working on my dissertation. I have told you I am crazy, but this may be the next level. But in all fairness, I am waiting to finish my dissertation until I can gather another set of data. So technically, I am in-between proposal and defense just hanging out, so what better way to pass the time than to write another book right? Ha right! Anyways, I am almost done with this whole Ph.D. journey thing, and I can't wait for it to be finished! But it has been a rough couple of years. And I'm not even talking about the course work (or STATISTICS!!). No, I'm speaking to the very first time I applied to the Ph.D. program I am in, and yes you read that correctly, the first time. Because I had more than one. Enter, my failure.

To set the stage, I had been working at the university for about 2 years. We were finally at a stable place in our department for me to not be doing my job in addition to another position. We had the help we needed, everyone was trained, ready to take on the new school year. I had sent in my application and was waiting to hear of my interview time. But it never came. Instead, I got a letter saying my application had not been accepted. First, I cried. A lot. Then I questioned how this was possible. Finally, I came to a place where I felt like a complete failure and figured I just wasn't good at anything anymore. It was a few years ago, I was a bit younger and a bit more dramatic ok. Forgive me. But seriously, how could it be possible that I wasn't accepted? I had an excellent essay, decent GRE scores, and strong recommendations. Or so I thought. I figured I should have at the very least been considered for an interview. But I wasn't. I didn't even get a phone call. After giving myself a few days of feeling lousy, I decided I was done feeling sorry for myself. I did something about it.

After I came back to the light from the darkness of feeling like a huge failure, I decided I would call the college my degree was in and figure out why I wasn't accepted. They always put in those letters a phone number to call if anyone ever has any questions and guess what? I DID have questions. Lots of them. But when I finally got on the phone with someone, I ended up only having two: Why was I rejected? And what can I do to improve my application for next time? Turns out my stellar application was missing something. Apparently, my recommendations spoke highly of me as a professional, but none spoke to my abilities as an academic. The committee had no idea how I would stand my ground in an academic setting, apart from what transcripts said about me. They needed more evidence from past professors to explain my work ethic in the classroom, my ability to think critically, and my willingness to do whatever it takes to be successful at research and academia.

Once I figured out what was wrong, I went back and gathered new recommendation letters, resubmitted my application and waited. As the Lord would have it, I was invited to an interview. I wish I could tell you I wow'ed the professors in my interview, but it was maybe the worst interview of my life. I had been used to excelling at professional interviews for jobs or internships, not for a place in a research-driven environment. I spent 30 minutes with the panel and walked out in tears. I was crying. AGAIN. I know you are so surprised. Now, after all I had done to make my application better and finally get an interview, it had gone horribly. You cannot imagine the level of failure I felt at that moment. I had now applied twice and was waiting for my second rejection to a program I thought was what the Lord wanted me to do. I was questioning if I had heard Him correctly. If this was really what He wanted for me? Because if this were His will, wouldn't it have been an easy and a smooth process? Wouldn't I have impressed the committee members and been accepted on the first application? Funny, God doesn't always work that way.

Actually, He rarely works things out smoothly by human standards. When you look at the Bible, you read stories of failure and how He has redeemed them. I want to point out two before going on with my failure story. First, we have Daniel. He is a highly regarded official and refuses to bow down to a king

or false god. He instead will only bow down to the
one, true God. For his stand, Daniel was thrown in a
den filled with hungry lions. So let's get this straight.
Daniel was doing what God had told him to do, and
he was being punished for it by the people the same
God put him in authority over? Yep. Lions don't
sound easy to me.

I mean my panel of professors were
intimidating, but they didn't bite off my head
(figuratively or literally). Daniel was obedient and still
had to go through something very scary. And it
wasn't just him! Something similar happened to his
friends, Shadrach, Meshach, and Abednego. They
were standing up for the Almighty God, but instead
of lions, they got the furnace. That's right. They
didn't face the beast, they had to face the fire. I would
have freaked out. But these guys boldly walked in the
flames believing God would somehow save them.
And even if God didn't save them, they knew they
had done the right thing. I don't know about you but
walking into a furnace does NOT sound easy or
smooth to me. It sounds awful and terrifying, let

alone hot! But God showed up! Not BEFORE they had to go into the fire, but God arrived and walked with them in the fire itself. You see, our big life moments, God always shows up. He is always there. It may not be smooth leading up to it, but in obedience, you will always end up where the Lord wants you to be. He will always redeem you.

I write all of this to say, I wish someone had reminded me of these men's' stories when I was going through the Ph.D. application fiasco. Then maybe I wouldn't have been so discouraged. Maybe I would have seen God in the fire with me rather than questioning if He was with me at all. Fire or not. At this point in the application process, I figured I was out. Like I said the interview was awful in my opinion and I wasn't worried about a spot in their program. I knew I wasn't worthy. I had failed myself. Then miracle of miracles (and it was definitely a miracle because I have no other idea how this happened) I got a letter in the mail that said I had been accepted and I started class in the Fall. I couldn't believe my eyes when I read that piece of paper. I was so excited and so thankful the Lord had somehow worked it all out. I ended up getting into the graduate program that fall semester with a zeal to prove to the committee members and to myself that I was meant to be there. That I had earned my place and that I wouldn't let them down and I definitely didn't want to feel like a failure again Which that statement is completely impractical, and little did I know the Ph.D. journey was designed for you to fail and learn from those failures. I had no clue what I was about to do to myself and my ability to manage failure.

The Lord worked it out, but it hasn't been smooth by my terms. I have battled other failures along the way, but He has remained faithful. There are times I have questioned his faithfulness, wondering if He knew what He was doing being faithful to someone like me. Didn't He know I was a mess? Didn't He know I didn't deserve His love, or encouragement, or grace? Wasn't He aware of how often I missed the mark? Yes, yes, yes, yes, and yes. He is 100% aware of all of those things. And crazy enough, He does it anyway. He loves me anyway. He has good things in store for me anyway. He works on my behalf anyway. His actions towards me are not dependent on my abilities or my successes. They are dependent on Himself and the actions of His son, Jesus. Everything I receive is because Jesus died for me and willingly gave me the freedom to walk in the light. And there is no way that can be taken away from me. As Romans 8:38-39 proclaims, "For I am sure that neither death nor life, nor angels nor rulers, nor things present nor things to come, nor powers, nor height nor depth, nor anything else in all creation, will be able to separate us from the love of God in Christ Jesus our Lord." Literally, there is nothing that can take us away from the Love of God. NOTHING. That is an overwhelming and unfathomable concept for me to grasp sometimes. But this weekend helped me a little bit.

I have spent the last two days loving on, laughing with and worshipping alongside some pretty amazing students. I volunteer in ministry with middle school girls at my church, and we spent this last weekend at a retreat, discipleship now, type of event.

The theme for the weekend was The Last Word, as in Jesus gets the last word in our lives. He gets the final say in defining who we are, in exploring our abilities and in determining our futures. He is the only one that offers us love, mercy, and grace without any strings attached. Over the weekend a few of the girls spoke to how the sessions encouraged them to understand more about how deep the Father's love was for them. They had never really understood what grace was and how faith worked.

One girl, in particular, spoke with me personally about her struggle with thinking awful thoughts about herself. She told me how she didn't know how to stop it, but that she often felt like she wasn't needed, she didn't matter to her friends, and that she ultimately didn't matter to Jesus. My heart broke for her! How terrible, as a young girl, to feel this way! And then I stopped because there are days I still feel like that and I'm 30! She said this weekend helped her have a stronger foundation in knowing God loved her no matter if she failed or messed things up. For the first time in her life, she felt like

God was with her and was taking care of her always. It was a beautiful hallelujah moment, and I was honored to be there to witness it. And even more excited to see how the Lord is going to use this moment to alter the course of her life.

Failing in the military isn't an option, though it can and does happen. If someone fails, missing their target, or fails the mission it is not good. The mistake or failure can sometimes have a very high cost in battle. This is why soldiers are trained to never fail, why they are trained until they are perfect. Thankfully, our heavenly Father took the price of failure away from us. It is no longer a burden we have to bear as believers. Instead, we are given a victory above all victories. We are part of the greatest accomplished mission this earth has ever seen.

Feeling like a failure is something we all face at countless points in our lives. Missing the mark is built into our DNA. We don't like to dwell on these experiences, but they tend to be the moments where we learn more about ourselves, our circumstances, and our abilities. As believers, we also learn more

about the characteristics of God and His greatness.
We get to see God flex His muscles. And there is
absolutely nothing we can do that will ever remove us
from His arms. Man, how awesome is that! This past
weekend has been a blessing to me, and one song
sums up what I have felt, what my middle schoolers
experienced, and what an abundant God we serve.

And oh, the overwhelming, never-ending,
reckless love of God.
Oh, it chases me down, fights 'til I'm found,
leaves the ninety-nine.
I couldn't earn it, and I don't deserve it.
Still, You give Yourself away.
Oh, the overwhelming, never-ending,
reckless love of God.

There's no shadow You won't light up
Mountain You won't climb up
Coming after me

There's no wall You won't kick down
Lie You won't tear down
Coming after me
-Cory Asbury, *Relentless Love*

I pray you will let the greatest love ever to be
known to fill your heart today. That you will know

with no doubt, your failures do not define your life nor determine your relationship with God. Instead, I pray you are reminded of the God you serve fights the battle with you, tears down walls for you, will leave everyone else behind to come to find you, and chases after you. Failures and all. There is absolutely nothing in this world or the heavens that will change that fact. Praise Him from whom all blessings flow! Every beautiful moment and blundering mistake. Praise Him all creatures here below. That is, every rock, animal, plant, organism, and man cry out His name. Praise Him above ye heavenly host. Not only us here on earth, but every entity in the heavens and galaxies will worship Him. Praise Father, Son, and Holy Ghost. Amen!

19
BRAVE IN THE BATTLE

I am a huge coward by nature. There are so many things I am fearful of. Some of them valid (like wild lions and snakes), others are simply fearing the unknown. Either way, being brave sounds so simple and yet it has brought me to my knees feeling incapable of just being in a brave stance. There are a variety of ways in which being brave comes into my everyday life. Some days it is the simple act of getting out of bed which requires me to be brave because I have to go through another day of being hurt by the words people say. Other days it is a feeling of facing the unknown on my own that brings the most fear. Right now, I am afraid of asking questions of the

Lord. Because if I ask the question, He is going to give me an answer. And what if the answer is too much? What if I can't do it? What if I'm not enough to make Him proud? What if... And yet, over and over again the Lord calls us to be brave, to take heart and have courage.

While I am scared of many things, I have found a few techniques that help me to stand up and be brave when it is necessary. First is through inspiration. It can come from anywhere, but inspiration is that spark that ignites in your soul and whispers "there is more out there, keep going." This comes to me from music, quotes, people, art, writing, scripture. Most recently inspiration has ignited in me from a movie, The Greatest Showman. This movie is not only one of incredible talent, but a message for all of us, that no matter our background, circumstance, or uniqueness beautiful things can happen if you follow your dreams and never give up. But it was also about braving the mockers, those who only want to beat you down. The musical score itself is by far one of the best out there and the anthem of the movie,

This is Me, echoes in my heart as I learn to be brave.
The chorus is a resounding reminder that just being
who you takes bravery.

I am brave
I am bruised
This is who I'm meant to be
This is me

Look out, cause here I come
And I'm marching on to the beat I drum
I'm not scared to be seen
I make no apologies
This is me

If you can read those lyrics and not be up on
your feet, shouting "THIS IS ME" then I'm not sure
you have blood pumping through your veins. Or
maybe you should listen to it for yourself and then
you'll be shouting. I promise. The point here is that
you find things that inspire you, that you seek them
out in the ordinary, daily life. And then you let them
grow your heart to a new level of bravery. Music can
be so empowering. Art, scripture, people. Take your
pick. But do pick something, small or large, ordinary
or extraordinary. Because sometimes being brave

needs a little boost.

The second way to be brave, especially in the thick of battle, is to surround yourself with encouraging people. I wrote a whole chapter on battle buddies, those that hold you accountable and help you be disciplined in your walk. Those same individuals will sharpen you to be brave as you egg each other on in battle. Have you ever been in the middle of hard workout, and you feel like stopping? Your mind is telling you there is no way your body can do one more burpee. It just can't. But then someone next to you says, "you're doing great" or "keep going" or "dig deep" or my personal favorite "Rachel, you have more in you." They are pushing you, encouraging and maybe even taunting you, to go just a little longer. There are few better feelings in the world to me than accomplishing just one more, proving to yourself and your partner you can do more than you believed was possible.

Achieving goals is literally one of my favorite things to do. It's super nerdy of me, but I'm pretty sure you all know me to be nerdy by now, and if you don't? The secret is out now. I LOVE conquering goals because it is a tangible thing I can go back and say, "look what I did!". Usually, I am only able to say that because the Lord has lavished grace upon my life, but it is still an amazing feeling to look back and see how far I have come. All because someone next to me encouraged me. In the thick of battle, when you are required to be brave, it is imperative you are surrounded with your battle buddy and others that will push you forward even if you are scared.

Another way I know how to conjure up bravery is to just fight for it. There will be plenty of days you won't be inspired or have the strength of those around you to encourage you forward. There will be some days it will just be you and God, and you will have to fight with every breath you have to be brave. I recently had some of those days. I felt as though the world wasn't on my side, my encouraging group of buddies was dealing with their own battles, and I was left to fight alone. Of course, as a believer, you are never alone. But sometimes it sure does feel like you are. Thankfully the Lord reminded me, He is all I need. Inspiration comes from Him. Even the benefit of others is a gift from God. So even though I find the strength to be brave from those things sometimes, it doesn't even come close to the boldness that comes from being in a close relationship with the Great High Priest, the Creator of the Universe, the King of Kings.

And there will be moments when the King is all I will have on my side. He will be the only cheerleader and the last inspiration. He tells us over and over. He will never leave us. And yet, we so easily forget. We depend on the people around us, we rely on ourselves, we seek music or food or whatever we can to fill the void. Hoping those things will make us stronger, more confident, braver. But ultimately, they don't. They will always fail us. They can't fill us. We know that, and we still seek them anyway until we finally figure out, they aren't enough. Not that we aren't enough, rather those items could never make us enough. There is only one person who can do that, and He is Jesus. He is the only one that can make us whole, and fully brave. Especially when we feel as though we are left all alone in a battle, we must find the will to just fight a little longer from the greatest Warrior that ever lived.

This calling, to just fight, is one of those things that is so very easy to type and incredibly difficult to live out. I feel like I'm writing a book full of those kinds of concepts. But you know what helps make it even the tiniest bit possible? He is already there making me exactly who I was always meant to be. Brave and bruised and all. My will to fight is being renewed. The Lord is making me brave even now. This is me. And this my friend, is you too.

20
WHEN THE ENEMY IS WINNING

The enemy we fight is the best there is. He is the Spartan for the ages, the Hercules of Hell, and the Dominator of Destruction. And there are just some days I feel like, and maybe you do too, that he is winning. There are days when the brokenness is extremely deep. My previous book called these sweatpants days. You don't think the world should continue as it is while you are still in such darkness. You feel as if you are a burden to yourself and those around you as you struggle to see the brighter side, experience renewed joy, even when you try to pick up your shield to fight the battle ahead. It is consuming and exhausting. When it feels as if the enemy is winning everything seems impossible. The littlest of tasks appear as mountains that are immovable. I mean where is the off button for this stuff? Sadly, I have found myself here many times over the last couple of months. Because even though I know the Lord is at work, it still seems like I am losing the fight, that somehow, I was forgotten. Do you ever feel this way?

I think there are three important things to know when you reach this depth of pain. The first being, YOU ARE NOT ALONE. When I am hurt, I tend to draw inwardly because the outside world has hurt me in some way. It is now untrustworthy in my heart, and I want to lick my wounds before heading back out to the war again. Being alone when you are hurt can be a good thing, and it can also be a VERY destructive thing. We are so good at telling ourselves lies, and if we are alone, no one is there to remind us of truth. The truth is a belt we wear around our waist, making sure our gut check is functioning properly. And that truth is: you are a child of the Most High King, the Creator of the Universe, He is always with you, and you are safe in His loving and gracious arms.

Not only are you His kid, but He is also a strong tower, a mighty warrior, and you need only to be still as He fights for you (Exodus 14:14). (Now repeat that to yourself over and over and over again until your heart and your head start to accept it. I'm right there with you speaking these truths over myself).

Next, the Devil is a flat-out liar. He will use anything and everything to destroy your spirit, your joy, and feed you to the wolves. I have seen him use circumstances, people I love, and even complete strangers to throw lies and twist words in my face that I am not good enough, I am unloved, and I will never be all that the Lord created me to be. You know how when you travel or are stressed and busy your immune system goes down? Once that happens you are likely to get sick even if you are someone who is usually extremely health. This is exactly what the Enemy does. When we are down, he comes in for the kill. EVERY. TIME. He uses every opportunity to get us to see why what he says is true about us.

Fighting this battle is probably one of the hardest for me. Because it feels like I am fighting

myself. I'm fighting my mind, all while trying to heal
my heart. And like I said before, I feel like I am alone
in this endeavor. Using that helmet of salvation is the
only thing I know of to fight this. Jesus uses
scriptures in the desert to fight the Devil. And if HE
has to use the Word to fight off the enemy, then you
better believe we need to. We need to use the Word,
surrounding our world with promises that are true
and reminders of the Lord's faithfulness. We also
need to speak the gospel over ourselves. Have you
ever done that before? It sounds weird I know. But I
think as believers we get so caught up in the good of
sharing the gospel with others that we forget to speak
it to ourselves. We forget that we too STILL need a
Savior. We need His mercies, His faithfulness and
love, and His cleansing of our hearts. This is
salvation. This is the good news. Remind yourself of
that. Start in 1 Corinthians 15. As you come to the
last two verses, I hope you hear a victory anthem
blasting in the background (Think Chariots of Fire or
the Hallelujah Chorus depending on your musical
style).

And the final important perspective to have in all of this is the very real notion that this is not the place the Lord, our Blessed Father, has called us to live in. We are not defeated. We may be pressed, but we are not crushed. Persecuted but not abandoned. Struck down but never destroyed. (And, yes, I'm singing the Delirious song in my head right now). He may have called you into a season of change that might be painful, but He has not called you to EVER live in defeat. He has already claimed victory over the entire dominion, do you really think you are so special you aren't included in that? That your heart is somehow left off the "entire dominion list"? If you are selfish like me, you may believe this lie sometimes, and say "yes I do think I was left off the list." Even typing that makes me feel like a whining toddler in the corner who didn't get their way. We are all there sometimes. I get it. TRUST ME. But that toddler stage is not where we are supposed to be. We are to walk in victory along with our Mighty Warrior. We are to claim our inheritance to His eternal throne and to march proudly through the valley until it becomes a mountain top.

I so wish I could tell you I'm an expert at this. I wish I could say that I am all about walking in victory and do so easily. But I don't. I am a struggling, imperfect being like everyone else. And I am constantly having to remind myself the truth of who I am and who God says He is. I'm still working on it. I am continually putting on courage and strength to fight the lies that incessantly try to seep into my brain. And I am here to tell you it is hard, but there is no more important battle you will face than the war over your heart and mind. It is the crux of your being, your soul, and your very life depends on it. The song below from Phil Wickham has been a balm to my heart as I seek perspective on what the Lord is doing. May it do the same for you. You are safe in His arms. Now pick up that shield, strap on your belt, and place the helmet on your head for the battle is raging. Our enemy is at large, but the victory is already claimed. I pray we will live and thrive in that truth. One dispelled lie at a time.

To the one whose dreams have fallen all apart
And all you're left with is a tired and broken heart
I can tell by your eyes you think you're on your own

But you're not alone
Have you heard of the One
who can calm the raging seas
Give sight to the blind, pull the lame up to their feet
With a love so strong it never lets you go
No, you're not alone

You will be safe in His arms.
You will be safe in His arms
The hands that hold the world are holding your heart
This is the promise He made,
He will be with you always
When everything is falling apart,
you will be safe in His arms

Did you know that the voice
that brings the dead to life
Is the very same voice that calls you now to rise
So, hear Him now, He's calling you home.
You will never be alone.

You will be safe in His arms.
You will be safe in His arms
The hands that hold the world are holding your heart
This is the promise He made,
He will be with you always
When everything is falling apart,
you will be safe in His arms

Cause these are the hands that built the mountains,
the hands that calm the sea
These are the arms that hold the heavens and
they are holding you and me
These are the hands that heal the leper

pull the lame up to their feet
These are the arms that were nailed to the cross to
break our chains and set us free

You will be safe in His arms.
You will be safe in His arms
The hands that hold the world are holding your heart
This is the promise He made,
He will be with you always
When everything is falling apart,
you will be safe in His arms
You will be safe
You will be safe
When everything is falling apart,
you will be safe in His arms

21
BATTLE-WORN

The thing about being a believer operating
with a wartime mentality means you are having to live
with the knowledge that there is always a war at hand.
Meaning, you are never really out of the war zone.
The mission is only complete when the Lord returns
for His final victory. This is a weighty calling.
Constantly living with a mission focused mindset can
be exhausting, maybe make you feel hopeless, or
worse make you fearful for the possibilities that may
come to pass (though won't because we know in the
end Jesus wins!). You will become battle worn. Your
body, mind, and spirit will be forever marked with the
missions you have completed and the failures you

have experienced. You feel as though you will never receive the rest or reset (R&R or furlough) you so desperately need in order to be effective in battle, think clearly and execute the commands given to you. I often feel as though I am battle worn. Do you?

I always know I've reached my most recent battle worn state when my prayers become pleas to the Lord for strength, I don't feel like I have anymore. I tell Him I'm tired of being strong, I'm tired of fighting what feels like a lost war, or I'm tired of fighting for others who don't seem to care about my sacrifice (finding themselves down range). The thing is these prayers, though incredibly true from my personal perspective of my own strength, are never actually the truth. The Lord quiets my tears and frustration and constantly says, "Come on dear one. Just take the next step. Keep going." You see, His perspective is so much grander and inclusive than mine is. His seat is so much higher, and His view is clearer than mine ever will be. My cries of exhaustion and frustration don't faze Him, because He knows just how close I am to His next act of faithfulness. He knows if I would just quiet my heart and breathe, He has the answer for me right around the corner.

Surviving in the battle-worn mindset is one thing, but let's go back to how you get there in the first place. Being battle worn means your resources have been depleted and you have reached the point where you are simply walking through the motions because the scars you bear have left no fight in you. It can also mean you are in a zombie state and the scars of past battles plague your mind. I don't know about you, but I'm super stubborn. I have been my whole life and Lord bless it He made me this way. He knows I'm bullheaded and want nothing more than to do things my own way. And that my friends, is exactly how I end up battle worn. I come to the battle prepared to depend on my own strength and resources rather than on the power and unending supply of grace that comes from our Mighty Warrior. And of course, I can't survive the battle on my own strength and failures invade the mission I've set out to complete alone. The war is way too big for me to be acting on my own. And yet I try to. So. Many. Times.

I have faith enough to believe I'm not the only one that does this.

Battle-worn is exhaustion from believing I could win on my own. But it is also being forever marked by the past you carry with you. It means your past has altered you and you now enter your current and future state with a different perspective because of what you have endured. This is not necessarily a bad thing. Often it is just the opposite. Battle-worn individuals tend to be the wise elders among our churches or the mature souls in our youth. They have seen and experienced both good and bad things that have forever changed their journey. Many times, they have no control over these experiences, but they have weathered them, and God has then been faithful to heal wounds and return them to their mission. While they may not return the same, their battle-worn hearts are a mark of God's great work in their lives. It is a badge of honor in a way that they have not given up. They have been faithful and run the race ahead of them. It also means they are among the "good and faithful servants" the Lord claims as His own today and every day of eternity.

Being battle-worn can also be a burden. In the military, there is a price all servicemen pay in order to fight for their country. Whether it is their time, youth, talents, or life itself, there is some kind of sacrifice being given. The mark of war on their lives then becomes a burden they will bear for the duration of their days. It may be a physical wound or a mental one. But however, it manifests itself in the solider, their battle-worn bodies are a sacrifice they have given for a cause. They are battle worn, and it has now become a burden rather than an honor. This type of battle-worn is one we should never take for granted. It has cost us a great deal to get to where we are in life. And whatever price was paid on the battlefield, has since changed their lives forever. They don't feel like a hero, but rather a survivor. A broken and beaten survivor.

So how do you endure the process of being or becoming a battle-worn soldier? Seek wisdom. You are not the first to go through this process, perishing through hard times or depending on your own strength to get you through to the end. There are many before you, and many more to come after you, that have survived this phase. Ask them for guidance. Listen to their story and be encouraged.

22
THE BROTHERHOOD

Have you ever experienced the bond that is
formed between fellow military members? They have
this special connection, regardless of background or
even rank; sometimes, they are bonded to each other.
They are a fraternity of sorts, having secrets among
them, seen things only they could know about, and
lived lives alongside one another through good and
bad. They are family, a band of brothers. This
brotherhood is a rare form of community that our
world desperately needs more of. As believers, we
also have the opportunity to belong to a brotherhood,
a community of believers, a church.

This may sound extremely simple, but the truth is we are kind of terrible at living in an authentic community. Most people believe living in a community means you have to share all your secrets with others, sit in awkward in conversations, and then never have time for other things because you are always "doing life" with this group. And to some degree, those are true but living in community means so much more. I will preface this chapter with a note, there are very few groups I have seen who do true community well. This is what contributes to the stereotypes mentioned earlier. It doesn't have to be awkward, though being vulnerable and your true self can sometimes feel awkward (usually because we aren't used to being our true self!). It will take time and require you to be intentional with those in your community. How else are you to build relationships without investing the time to do so? And while everyone is scared to share the darkest parts of themselves, I have found it to be more freeing than frightening. But it is still a burden, to share your sin with others. They take on part of the burden, and you will take on part of the burden for theirs. This is the brotherhood.

If it takes so much time and is so awkward, why is living in a community so important? Well first, God never intended for us to try and do this Christian life alone. Hebrews 10:24-25 reminds us "And let us consider how to stir up one another to love and good works, not neglecting to meet together, as is the habit of some, but encouraging one another, and all the more as you see the Day drawing near." He designed us to live in a community, for most of us to be married, and for us all to participate in fellowship on a congregational level. None of those things can happen reading your bible in your house alone. Reading your bible is important, but it is not all He has for us. Community is meant to be a great gift from God, in order to live a rich and challenging life together. It is meant to bring us joy, not frustration, freedom, not condemnation. It takes us beyond the casual "hello" in the sanctuary, and into the world of "what is going on in your life and how can I be praying for you." Living in community is not casual, it is intentional.

It is meant to be a safe place to discuss things you don't understand about God, the Bible, Jesus, the Holy Spirit, life in general. Just this past week in our small group we are reading through Hebrews and came across Melchizedek and his priesthood. I don't know how theologically savvy you are, but for me, the whole Melchizedek thing does not make sense to me. In Hebrews 7, it talks about how he lives forever, is not of the priesthood line to rule, and his name actually means "king of righteousness." Wait, what? Aren't those things meant to describe Jesus? But this guy isn't Jesus? Then who is he, and why does he sound so much like Jesus? And if he is so great, why isn't he mentioned more often in the bible? Ugh. See what I mean. It is confusing! You read it and let me know what you think. I'm totally ok with not knowing all the answers because I believe Christ will reveal those things to us at the right time whether on earth or in heaven. But still, I think it is healthy to ask the questions, to discuss and sometimes debate, because it makes me think. Small groups, or community, is one of the best places for this type of thing.

This group of believers is also to serve as a source of accountability and wisdom. I like to surround myself with good people, wise people, life-giving people. This small group should be that for you. You are all cut from the same cloth of love. You have the same foundation. There may be disagreements on some things, but the big foundational elements of life should be something you agree on. From that foundation, you are then able to build a life of accountability with one another. I spent an entire chapter talking about accountability, calling them your battle buddies. When you are facing a life battle, these are the people on your right and left. They are the prayers you cherish, the wisdom you seek, and the guidance you listen to. Hopefully, these community members know you well, so that when advice is sought, you know it is coming from a place of love and concern.

The brotherhood we are given the opportunity to be a part of is a way for us to live out the gospel, loving God and loving others. Ecclesiastes says it so beautifully, "Two are better than one because they have a good reward for their toil. For if they fall, one will lift up his fellow. But woe to him who is alone when he falls and has not another to lift him up! Again, if two lie together, they keep warm, but how can one keep warm alone? And though a man might prevail against one who is alone, two will withstand him—a threefold cord is not quickly broken." (4:9-12). This is one of my favorite verses and encouragements for doing life with other believers. Because when I fall, and I will fall, they are there for me. Together we are not easily broken. One of my military friends reminded me that missions are successful because of a team, never because of one individual person. The same is true of our Christian lives. We are successful in this battle, in this mission, because we are given a brotherhood (or sisterhood) to depend on along with the gifts Christ has blessed us with.

These are just a few benefits for living in the brotherhood of believers. I didn't even touch on the church itself, which would take an entire book in itself. There is so much more out there for you to know and understand about living in community. There are great resources available in the Christian community. However, at the end of the day, it is important to remember this is guidance the Lord has placed on our lives. If you aren't living in a Christian community, I urge you to start. Reach out to your church and ask them about small groups or a Sunday school class you can get involved in. It will most likely be awkward. It will definitely take time, maybe even a long time for you to find the best people for you to do life with. But it will be worth it. My life is better because of accountability, my small group, and the ministry teams I am able to serve on. These groups of people are invested in my life, and I am invested in theirs. It is such a gift. It means I get to share my burden with someone, get to celebrate life's victories together, as well as cry through the tragedies together. It is a constant, physical reminder of God's love for me, and the blessings He has given to me in my earthly life. I pray you are able to find your people and you challenge one another. Love your squad fiercely. It will be worth every uncomfortable conversation and every minute of your time.

23
THE PRICE OF FREEDOM

You know that saying, "the best things in life are free"? Yeah, that one. Who came up with that? It is the biggest lie I have ever heard. The best things in life are not free. Family is free, as in you are born into it, but having intentional relationships with your family is NOT free. It costs you time, being uncomfortable, maybe even some money to be near them. It takes some form of investment. Love is definitely not free. It may be freely given by some people, but even that cost the giver something. Love has a price tag associated with it. The question is, are you willing to pay the price? Well, my friends, our freedom has come at a very high price.

In all the world wars that have gone on in the last century alone, nearly half a million US soldiers have died paying the ultimate price for freedom of this country. And there are thousands more who may not have lost their lives, but they lost relationships with their family members, they lost a limb or lost their sense of normal. All gave some, but some gave all. They all gave something, if not everything, to defend freedom for this country. That is a HUGE price to pay. They lived out the greatest example of love, to lay down their life for their brothers, both known and unknown. Our personal freedoms in this country have been bought with a price of blood. Lots and lots of blood. The same is true of our spiritual freedoms. They were bought with blood. All it took was blood from one man, Jesus. He was the only one needed to pay the price for all of our freedom from condemnation.

Ok so this word condemnation, what is it? It sounds SUPER churchy and it kind of is. I never knew what it meant growing up. I just thought it

sounded bad, evil almost. And I guess it kind of is.
Well here's what Webster's dictionary says is the
official definition of condemnation "the expression of
very strong disapproval, censure, the action of
condemning someone to a punishment, sentencing."
So yeah it doesn't sound awesome at all. To these
people pleasing person (we've talked about this- I'm
still working on it!), the words "very strong
disapproval" make me want to curl up in a ball and
cry. There may not be a more painful way to hurt me
than with disapproval or disappointment. Ouch. But
seriously. It is the WORST! And it makes me want to
dance down the street singing Hallelujah at the top of
my lungs that Jesus has saved me from this
disapproval!

I know you are wondering how this is even
possible. Well, my friend, I am so glad you asked. The
easy answer is because God is AMAZING. Period.
But for those of you who need a little bit more and
don't have the childlike faith you are called you
have... ha just kidding, I just wanted to add a
Christian jab in there somewhere. Anyways, where

was I? God is amazing. Yes! Not only that but He had this whole crazy, ornate thing planned out well before the foundations of the earth were laid. Before people ever walked this earth, before animals were a thing, and way before Jesus was a growing baby in Mary's womb. Long before all of history, God knew this world would be messed up (Thanks, Eve!) and that in order for us to be with Him one day there would need to be something to stand in the gap. Because there was a really, REALLY big sized gap that needed to be filled.

Before Jesus was here, that gap was bridged by animal sacrifices and lots of rules. The Old Testament outlines many rules God placed on His people if they wanted to be considered holy and blameless before Him. They couldn't eat pork. They had to kill bulls a certain way and sprinkle their blood in a specific manner in order to present a pleasing aroma to Yahweh. I have always wondered if I could have handled being alive when sacrifices were part of everyday life as a believer. I mean if you have read through any of the Old Testament, there is blood all over the place. No thank you! Enter Jesus.

When the New Testament opens up in Matthew, we see a new form of sacrifice take place. In society, this has not replaced the sacrifices going on in the temple yet, but we see the life of the one who will become the ultimate sacrifice. We see Jesus become man, worship in the temple, and begin his ministry here on earth at the age of about 30. We are going to pause here for a second. I turned 30 this past year. I know you are completely shocked at how wise I am despite my limited years… right? Anyways, I turned 30 this past year. I planned an amazing trip where I got to ride an elephant, lay down with tigers, and zip line through the jungle. It was one of the best things I have ever done in my life. I wanted to start my third decade off with a huge success. Before I laid my head down to sleep that first night of being in my thirty's, I thought when Jesus was my age he was about to enter into a world and do miraculous things. He also was heading into the beginning of the end of his life, and he knew it.

He started his ministry at a wedding, the

pinnacle of celebrations, the start of a new life together for the married couple, a joyous occasion. Three years later he would end his time on earth through the most horrific of deaths. And he knew it all along. I don't know if the Wedding at Cana was around his birthday or not, but it was a large shindig, kind of like riding elephants. Jesus entered his third decade with a bang knowing it was leading to the cross in a very short time. He lived his life EVERY DAY with that knowledge. Can you imagine? You know when you are getting ready to go on vacation or start a new chapter? You count down the days until that new thing or adventure happens right? I always wonder, did Jesus do the same? Did he count down his days on earth because he knew they were numbered? I have to believe he did because everything he did was with great intentionality. He lived with a wartime mentality every second of every day of his 33 years here on earth.

We talked more about wartime mentality in another chapter, but I put this here to call attention to the fact that when I turned 30, I felt a different connection with Jesus that I had never felt before. I felt very young in comparison to the wisdom and ministry that was in Jesus at 30 years of age. I would have been scared out of my mind. But Jesus wasn't. He was ready. He had been preparing for this day his entire life. So back to his ministry. He healed sickness, cast out demons, called out the truth, resisted the Devil, calmed the storm, walked on water, fed thousands, loved people, and saved the world all in 3 years. No big deal. What I think we sometimes forget being on this side of his journey to the cross is, the ministry of Jesus cost him greatly. He was constantly away from his family in order to pursue the hearts of others all over the area. He was widely unpopular among the people in power. He was spit on, mocked, and ridiculed repeatedly for being different from the cultural norms. He was basically a homeless man dependent on the charity of others. Nowhere in the Bible does it say, and after completing his daily ministry, Jesus went home to his white picket fence neighborhood to spend quality time with his family and eat a lavish meal. Jesus sacrificed comfort, status, and ultimately his life for our freedom.

So, what is this freedom then? What does it look like? And how in the world do we accept this gift and live in freedom? Dear friends if you get nothing from this book, I pray you get this one thing. Our freedom, which was paid for by the blood of Jesus Christ, is meant to be a peace and assurance we have in knowing we are no longer under rules and regulations, animal sacrifices and ceremonial occasions. Instead, we are called to live in freedom from these restrictions. Freedom from having to do things a certain way to reach God. We need only to accept the gift of Christ as our Savior in order to be made blameless and righteous in the eyes of God. Our disapproving lives are no longer seen as such, rather we are seen as clean and whole because we were paid for with the ultimate blood offering. We are approved (PRAISE THE LORD!!!) because of him who set us free.

Living in freedom comes with responsibility. As the saying goes, "to whom much is given, much is required." This saying, I 100% agree with. Living in freedom does not give us the right to act a fool.

Though, we all have our moments. Living in freedom means we have the responsibility to uphold the values and character of the one who gifted freedom to us. Out of respect, we are to dedicate our lives to protecting and spreading this freedom to the world. It is our duty to instill this concept to the next generation and build them up to be strong believers of the faith and defenders of our freedom in Christ. The price of freedom for this country always costs someone something. The price of eternal freedom is freely given to us through Jesus, we need only to accept it and then share it to the masses. That is the price of freedom.

24
MISSION ACCOMPLISHED

There isn't a feeling quite like finishing a race, completing a goal, or winning a game. Victory is something we all want in our lives, even if it is the only victory over the day we are currently living. From what I understand, accomplishing a mission often feels the same. You've done the job you set out to do and have returned to give your report. This same mentality can be applied to our mission as believers- to spread the good news and do kingdom work. And at the very end, we get to share in the victory of accomplishing the mission. But there's a long road between now and our victory party in heaven. What, then, can we do between now and then to help accomplish the mission? Friend, you ask such amazing questions!

Scripture describes our mission in a variety of ways, a race to the finish, seeds to plant, or a field to harvest. Notice how none of these descriptors are passive, all are active. Meaning, there is work to be done. I don't know about you, but I dislike running. So, the idea of running a race and finishing just sounds terrible. But when I apply it to watching the Olympics, I'm all about it! I am cheering those athletes on, wanting them to go as hard as they possibly can for that finish line and win the medal. Have you seen those athletes? They put everything they have into their training, but once the race has begun the only thing that matters is breathing and crossing that line. Pushing themselves with everything in them to get them to the end. Can you imagine what that same image would look like if we applied it to spreading the gospel? Thankfully we have some good examples. Two, in particular, stand out to me across history.

The first Jesus athlete I think of that lived in

modern day is Billy Graham. Mr. Graham was an evangelist for his entire life. He died earlier this year (2018) just shy of his 100th birthday. This man saw a lot of the world, spoke to people from every generation and tribe, touched millions of lives, and brought even more to know the name of Christ. His entire mission in life was to share Jesus with anyone he met or would listen to him. He spoke with kings, queens, presidents, religious and political leaders, along with normal people like you and me. He was one of the first preachers to utilize media, TV, and radio, to reach people for the name of Jesus. He was named one of the ten most admired men in the world by the Gallup organization 51 times over his lifetime. Long before he passed away, he became known as "America's Pastor."

This man had the accolades to make him famous, but the heart that made him sincere. And he spent his entire life giving the glory to God. He wasn't a perfect man, no one is. But if you are looking for an example, someone just like you and me, who never had the privilege of physically seeing Jesus walk the earth, but who ran the race ahead of them with extreme strength, and accomplished the mission set before him, Billy Graham is your man. He would get a gold medal. And he is celebrating the victory with Christ right now, for all eternity. And you know what else? I bet he is now meeting some of those who came to know Christ through his ministry for the first time. How beautiful!

Now I'm not saying you have to have a TV show or a radio segment to be a gold medalist for the Kingdom, though how cool would that be! What I am saying is if Billy, who was born on a dairy farm in Charlotte, North Carolina can help reveal the light and love of Jesus to millions, so can you. What is holding you back? What is it that is keeping you from reaching millions, or just reaching the person you work next to? The girl who babysits your kids? The family member who just hangs on to their unbelief? Maybe it is fear. Fear of rejection, fear of failure, fear of not having all the answers. The thing is if we let fear be our guide in life, we would never do anything. Seriously, we couldn't even sit and watch TV for fear of the screen catching on fire, or fear of the show being a waste of time (which man there are so many of those!). While all of those excuses sound ridiculous, you get my point. When fear is our compass, we are held captive. The first step in accomplishing our mission is to not let fear rule our lives. Rather, we overcome our fear by seeking the fearless one, the Lion of Judah, Jesus.

Jesus has been used for countless examples in this book already (which should be the case!), but to me, the most important example He has for us is in accomplishing the mission. We can argue all you want about this not being the most important example. I think, however, everything He did on this earth was all part of His cross-ward journey, aka accomplishing His mission. Every characteristic He displayed, every sermon He gave, every person He healed, all of it was so He could be one day closer to finishing His mission here on earth.

One characteristic of Jesus that I admire the most during those final days, from Palm Sunday to Easter morning, was His ability to be fully present.

He knew exactly what was ahead of Him. He knew the cheers would soon become slander, the palms would turn to whips, and the donkey would be a cross. He knew! And yet, reading through the Bible about His arrival into town, I get the feeling He was happy. Maybe He was smiling along with His friends, enjoying the warm welcome, basking in the light of His Father. And then even more so in the upper room with His disciples, His friends. He sat with them, ate with them, washed their feet (EVEN JUDAS'), was 100% present with His crew.

John 13:1 says it beautifully, "Now before the Feast of the Passover, when Jesus knew that his hour had come to depart out of this world to the Father, having loved his own who were in the world, he loved them to the end." You see those last 6 words. He loved them to the end. He knew Judas would betray Him, knew Peter would deny Him, knew some of His disciples would leave Him, and knew His death was days away. And still, He loved them. All of them. Y'all, I don't know about you, but if I knew I was in my final days and KNEW I was surrounded by crappy people who would abandon me in my time of need, I WOULD NOT HAVE STAYED THERE. That's right. I wouldn't have eaten dinner with them, I definitely wouldn't have washed their feet. I would not have wanted to waste a single second of my last days with people like that. You can call me names all you want, but would you? Would you stay surrounded by people that were going to hurt you if you KNEW they were going to hurt you? The answer is no. If we could avoid hurt, we would almost every time. Especially emotional hurt. Physical hurt some people say they can get over and it will heal. But emotional hurt lingers long after the incident. And I just wouldn't have stuck around to endure that in my final days.

I'm not Jesus. SHOCKER! And PRAISE THE LORD! Instead of running for the hills to spend time alone crying His eyes out because death was coming, He loved them to the very end. This cuts a knife right through my heart. In a good way. Because if Jesus, who is about to face a brutal and gruesome death can love betrayers and liars until His last breath, I can find the courage to be present in the world around me. Or to speak kindly to those around me. Or I can be more open to letting Him use me in situations. Because He loved me with His everything, I can love others with all I have.

I am writing this chapter on Easter Sunday. The significance of that is not lost on me. Today is the day we have celebrated the tomb did not hold our Savior, death did not get the last say, and Jesus accomplished His mission of making a way for us to join Him in the final victory. Before Jesus could get to Easter Sunday, He had to go through Good Friday. He endured so much that day. Beatings, whippings, thorns, ridicule, nakedness, betrayal. He went through the worst day EVER. And there He was, nailed to a cross, surrounded by criminals, left to die. Then came His final moments. John 19:28-30 says, "After this, Jesus, knowing that all was now finished, said (to fulfill the Scripture), "I thirst." A jar full of sour wine stood there, so they put a sponge full of the sour wine on a hyssop branch and held it to his mouth. When Jesus had received the sour wine, he said, "It is finished," and he bowed his head and gave up his spirit." Knowing that all was now finished, all was accomplished, then and only then did Jesus give up His spirit. And even then, that wasn't the end.

No, Sunday was coming. He knew it, but no one else did. He was very aware of how this story would go. He would die and then be raised again so that we would serve a God who kept His promises. I love it when people keep their promises to me. It builds my trust in them, increases their integrity, and continues to remind me there is still hope in this crazy world for people to keep their word. The same is true of my relationship with God. I trust Him because He does what He says He will do. He doesn't go back on His word, doesn't lie to me or play games with me. He isn't out to manipulate me or humiliate me. He keeps His word every single time. And He did just that through Jesus and giving Jesus the ability to accomplish His mission. To love others until the end and finish what He started- making a path for us to be with Him forever in Heaven.

Friends, this Easter I have been reminded of

how gracious God is to me. And how often (which is frequently) I feel unworthy of that grace. But then Romans 8:11 gets thrown in there, and my feelings are silenced. Romans 8:11 says, "The Spirit of God who raised Jesus from the dead lives in you." (insert the sound of crickets now!). Seriously though, the Spirit of God is no joke. He is powerful, mighty, courageous, intelligent and completely capable. And Romans is saying that same EXACT spirit that took Jesus from death to life, from dead to risen lives in me. IN ME. That is just so crazy amazing. I mean really? Does it get any better?

I can love until the end, I can live without fear, I can run full speed ahead to accomplish the mission because He is in me. If He can raise the dead, He can surely get this anti-athlete across the finish line. And that is what I want to do. Love others until the very, very end and know that I have given all to accomplishing His mission here on earth. Boy, do we have our work cut out for us! "But God raised him from the dead, freeing him from the agony of death because it was impossible for death to keep its hold on him." Acts 2:24. Nothing can hold us back. Not the chaos of this world, nor even the finality of death, is an impossible circumstance for God. Your mission is not impossible. Your mission is accomplishable because He lives in you.

FINAL THOUGHTS

Friends, thank you so much for coming on this journey with me. You have no idea how honored I am you spent your time and energy on this labor of love. I am praying that the Lord has used this resource as a way to encourage your heart and increase your faith. That you would find the courage and strength to stand firm in any and every battle you may face in your life, and most importantly to know you are not alone. We are all in this crazy mess together, encouraging one another with our words and actions, and being held up by the grace of our amazing Heavenly Father. You are so loved and so brave. I pray you will always take that truth with you wherever you go.

My first book, *Sweatpants & Stilettos*, was written out of a season of trials. There was so much learning I did as a person during that time and I was encouraged writing my story in the hope others would find it as a loving friend and caring sister in Christ. This book, however, has been out of a beautiful season of triumph. I'm not saying there were consistent victories all the time, more like my attitude about trials has shifted in the last few years. What I previously saw as heartbreaking, I now see as disappointing and sometimes sad but not devastating. What I would have responded to in anger and frustration, I now look at through a lens of love and mercy (most of the time anyway). The Lord has been gracious to grow me in ways I didn't even realize until I put it all into a narrative until I was able to pour it out onto these pages. He has been so kind to me. I do not know all the answers, nor do I know what my future looks like. What I do know is as warriors, our victory is guaranteed, and our commander in chief is leading us toward that final victory.

The war is at hand, the warriors are few, and there is much ground to cover. Be brave. Be ready. You are the soldiers He has called out to be among His victors. And it is now time for you to take these weapons and wield them for His kingdom and your good. I can't wait to see what you do with these tools. I'm so excited to know how the Lord uses you for His work in the lives of your family members, your friends, your coworkers, your neighbors, and your communities. You are the light. You are the foot soldiers of the Lord's Army, and I'm so thankful for the opportunity to rage war with you.

Music has been in my life forever. And you can tell from previous chapters, it inspires me, makes me think, and refocuses me all the time. So, you know I can't say goodbye without leaving you a song. This one is a bit older than some of the others (it is from an actual hymnal!), but sometimes the oldies are the goodies.

Like a mighty army, Moves the Church of God;
Brothers, we are treading, Where the Saints have trod.
We are not divided; All one body we:
One in hope and doctrine, One in charity.

Onward Christian soldiers, Marching as to war
With the cross of Jesus, Going on before

Onward, then, ye people; Join our happy throng.
Blend with ours your voices, In the triumph song:
Glory, laud, and honor, Unto Christ, the King.
This through countless ages, Men and angels sing.

Onward Christian soldiers, Marching as to war
With the cross of Jesus, Going on before
-Onward, Christian Soldiers, verses 3 & 4

Let us not be divided. Let us not grow weary. Instead let us march on as to war, with a wartime mentality, using all the tools God has bestowed upon us, knowing Christ has gone before us, and the final victory is ours because of Him. Onward, friends and fellow soldiers.

All my love and best,

Rachel

ABOUT THE AUTHOR

Rachel is a lover of Jesus, education, music, DIY projects and travel. She spends her days helping people make goals and achieve their dreams, and her nights kickboxing, reading, cooking good food, enjoying time with friends and family, and planning her next traveling adventure. She lives in Dallas and is honored to be the aunt of four nieces and two nephews.

Made in the USA
Columbia, SC
08 July 2019